POSITIVE
CASH FLOW

POSITIVE CASH FLOW

COMPLETE CREDIT AND COLLECTIONS FOR THE SMALL BUSINESS

Establishing a credit policy

Avoiding bad checks and credit cards

Keeping track of overdue accounts

Specific pointers and wording for effective collection letters

What to say during collection phone calls

How to respond to objections and stalls

When to resort to collection agencies, attorneys or court

Legal guidelines you must follow

GINI GRAHAM SCOTT, Ph. D.

BOB ADAMS, INC.
PUBLISHERS

Holbrook, Massachusetts

This publication is designed to provide accurate and authoritative information with regard to the subject matter covered. It is sold with the understanding that the publisher is not engaged in rendering legal, accounting, or other professional advice. If legal advice or other expert assistance is required, the services of a competent professional person should be sought.

Published by Bob Adams, Inc., 260 Center Street, Holbrook, Massachusetts, 02343.

Printed in the United States of America.

ISBN: 1-55850-900-3

Dedication

To M.M, S.T., R.G., R.K., H.N, and all the rest.

Acknowledgments

Grateful thanks must be extended to Kate Layzer and Elizabeth Tragert for their assistance with this project.

Contents

INTRODUCTION: The Difficulty of Collecting Debts

For many people, the process of successfully collecting debts is a mystery. You ask for the payment you have coming, the debtor gives you an excuse, and you don't know what to say next. How do you avoid this situation?

Many creditors give up on collecting debts before they should because they fear the debtor's ill will. Some stop trying because they assume the debtor is a won't-pay deadbeat who has no money, when this is not the case. Still others give up because they aren't aware of the legal remedies available to them, and don't know how to show the debtor they are really serious.

On the other hand, some creditors become so emotionally involved and pursue their debt so energetically that they may actually end up owing the debtor money when the debtor sues for libel, slander, harassment, theft, assault, extortion, or other illegal collection practices.

If you want to collect the money people owe you, you need to know the rules of the collection game; you can then be creative within these general guidelines. Indeed, in many instances, it is necessary to be resourceful; you will be competing with other creditors for payment from a debtor who doesn't have enough to pay everyone, or who uses a priority system to pay the more important debts first. In that case you have to find a way to make your claim come to the top of the pile--or perhaps look for nonmonetary alternatives to getting paid.

Of course, collecting what you are owed is only half the story. The other half involves taking preventive measures in advance to protect yourself from collection problems. Depending on circumstances, these measures can range from writing up effective loan agreements to making decisions about when to extend credit and to whom. A strong credit policy will help you decide under what circumstances you will extend credit--and how much you will risk.

Credit–Everywhere You Look

Remember, anytime you make an exchange with anyone and don't immediately get cash, you are extending credit. And that includes working for someone, accepting a check (in reality a promise to pay), billing someone for a product or service, or making a loan.

If you think about it, you'll realize that every society operates on some form of credit. Even a simple society that uses barter instead of money incorporates a credit system. Say a person performs some activity for another, such as working in a field sharing food from a hunt. That activity establishes a debt whereby the other person is expected to perform some reciprocal action in return--perhaps doing work in the future or sharing later from his own supply of food.

Thus, credit is, in a sense, the grease that keeps the wheels of society moving. Credit facilitates relationships: not every transaction can be immediately concluded with a payment in money, services, or products in return. But because the parties to a transaction agree or expect that reciprocal activity or payment will occur at or by a certain time, they can proceed with business.

In any situation where you extend credit, you have to determine an acceptable risk level. You must also realize that you are making a trade-off between your investment of time and energy in the transaction and your expectation of getting paid. In effect, there is a trade-off between sales and credit; if enough people refuse to buy from you without credit, your conviction that you are "saving" money by refusing credit to your customers may come back to haunt you.

Extending credit can indeed increase the likelihood of making a sale. But there is always the matter of getting paid, and the very act of extending credit brings with it a measure of risk--however small--that payment will not be forthcoming. Accordingly, you must weigh the value of making a transaction that can increase your business, help a friend, or strengthen a relationship with the possibility that you will not receive the expected payment.

Being too conservative in extending credit can lose you sales (or even put a crimp in some of your personal relationships, though personal borrowing is not the province of this book). On the other hand, being too liberal can create severe financial problems for you and possibly lead to a business or personal bankruptcy. You must strive for a balance that works for you and decreases your risks by maximizing the chances that you will effectively collect the money people owe you.

How This Book Will Help You

This book is designed to help you collect this money in two ways. First, it will help you establish a good credit policy so you can make the best decision about whether to extend credit (in the form of money, work, or sales). And second, it will help you in determining exactly what to do when you have problems collecting after you have extended credit.

Positive Cash Flow takes into consideration that your strategies for extending credit and collecting will differ depending on the debtor's individual characteristics and personality. The book also deals with the legal niceties of what you can and cannot do when you try to collect--so you don't end up owing more than you're owed.

While this book is designed especially for the small business person owed a small amount of money (up to about $2,000) individuals or business people who are owed much more should find the basic principles and strategies discussed in this book useful as well.

CHAPTER 1:
Establishing Your
Financial Policy

Whenever you aren't paid in full in cash immediately, you are extending credit. This always involves some risk. The check may not clear; the account may be closed; the debtor may not pay your bill, or may take too long to pay.

To protect yourself and reduce risks, you need to create a preventive financial policy with guidelines on when to give credit, under what conditions, and whom to give it to.

It's important to have your own clearly thought-out policy. If you don't, you will tend to make decisions on the spur of the moment, or end up going along with whatever the other person's policy happens to be. With your own policy, you have your own standards. You can still be flexible, varying your policy to cover a number of situations with different people. The crucial thing is to have a policy you can adapt to suit your own needs, and to understand the trade-offs and risks this policy brings with it.

Depending on circumstances, you can then use one predetermined credit arrangement or another. And if people question why you're so tough, you can always blame it on your accountant or attorney: "My accountant wants us to have everyone fill out this form when we offer credit."

Without your own established policy, it's easy to let someone control you based on his or her own needs. This often creates serious problems. Perhaps you've heard the old business school joke: "You set the price; I'll set the terms."

Your customer, client, or friend may try to pay you as little as possible over as long a period as possible. Perhaps you send someone a bill, and he pays you 60 days later, saying, "That's the way we normally pay." Perhaps that's true; nevertheless, you wanted your money within 10 days, and you didn't get it. You must establish such matters in advance.

You'll have more leeway to set your own standards when you deal with individuals and small companies. Big companies are often locked into standard billing cycles and may require several approvals to approve even a small payment. However, you can often cut through this red tape if you are insistent--and you may even be able to get payments in advance.

Some Considerations in Setting Your Policy

With a solid, established credit policy, you don't have to engage in guesswork when the credit situation arises; you know what to do. In setting up such a policy, you need to determine in advance your answers to questions like these:

(1) Do I expect all payments to be in cash, money order, or C.O.D., or will I extend credit?

(2) How large a deposit do I want before doing any work or shipping products? Then, when the job is completed or the product shipped, do I want cash only? Will I accept C.O.D., or will I bill?

(3) Will I accept checks, and if so, for how much, and what identification or verifications will I need?

(4) Will I accept credit cards, and if so, which ones? What kind of credit checks will I make to protect myself?

(5) What contract forms do I need to cover the situations likely to occur in my business? What kind of protective clauses do I want in these contracts to cover me if I am not paid?

(6) When I bill, what kind of terms will I offer? What discounts, if any, will I give for early payments? What charges for interest or penalties will I add if payments are late? And when will these charges start?

By the same token, you must determine when you will start charging for your products and services, and make sure that your customer or client knows your policy. For example, some lawyers and consultants offer their first hour or half-hour of consulting free, so that the client can decide whether he or she wants their services. Others charge immediately--and some want payment in cash or check right after the consultation. Others even ask for full payment before the session starts.

Any number of credit policies may work for your business. The main idea is to set your policy beforehand, not to create it on the spur of the moment. In this way, you have a clear rationale for your policy, and you will appear decisive when you let your customer or client know what it is.

Policies may differ widely, because business situations, customers, clients, and products or services differ. You may even want to have different policies to cover different situations.

For instance, many marketing consultants who work with large companies don't charge at their first meeting with a client. This is because the first hour is essentially a sales pitch that may result in a contract for many hours of work. On the other hand, marketing consultants dealing with small, start-up companies are more likely to charge (perhaps in advance) for an initial meeting. In this case, the customers might need an hour or two of advice to establish direction or resolve marketing problems before tackling remaining issues on their own. You may even have alternate credit policies for different customers, depending on your assessment of the customer's ability and willingness to pay.

Establishing a more rigorous financial policy may result in losing some customers or clients. On the other hand, it may be to your advantage to lose those people who don't like to sign contracts or make firm commitments. The key question is not just how much you sell or what work you do--but how successfully you can collect.

The Link Between Credit and Sales

As we've noted, in setting your financial policy, you must consider the link between credit and sales. Sometimes the two can conflict, since a tough credit policy can discourage sales. A more liberal policy, on the other hand, can often be used as a competitive tool to promote your products or services, and induce people to buy. For example, some speakers who sell books at their lectures have signed on as merchants with MasterCard or Visa; many attendees don't want to pay cash, don't have their checkbooks, or don't want to write a check, but will make a purchase if there is an opportunity to buy on credit.

Similarly, many suppliers know they'll get more clients and make more sales if they extend credit. For example, a start-up company may choose a printer to print its brochures because the printer doesn't require a deposit up front, agrees to take less down, or gives the company longer to pay. In this case, if the start-up is strapped for cash, the credit the printer extends is a sales incentive to choose that printer over another--even if the actual bid is the same or a little higher. If the new business goes well, the printer's decision may lead to more work from that customer in the future.

However, for every opportunity there is also a risk. Credit losses for businesses are now about five percent of sales on the average, compared to only two to percent a few years ago. In some industries, bad debt levels are even higher. Clearly, this problem is something that must be taken into account in weighing the risks.

Remember, every loss means you must work that much harder or sell that much more in order to compensate, depending upon your average profit margin. For example, if you've got a margin of 10 percent, for every $100 loss you suffer, you have to sell another $1,000 in products or services to catch up.

The Risks of Extending Credit

The risks of extending credit take various forms. For instance, a customer who buys your product or service on MasterCard or Visa can always return the product or dispute the bill, and if successful, the purchase will be charged back to you. Another risk is that the company to whom you extend credit can go belly-up.

If you're in a company that's big enough to have different people handling credit and sales, realize that the two should ideally be coordinated. For example, your salesperson can casually pick up credit information in the course of making a sale, because he or she already has the customer's good will, and the customer will probably be more receptive to the idea of offering information to the salesperson. When someone else calls for a credit check, the person might get suspicious and defensive.

On the other hand, salespeople often need a tight leash to make sure they don't offer too much credit to make the sale; all too often, cavalier salespeople deliver customers who simply can't pay. Whatever your situation, you should have a credit policy already worked out--and you should coordinate it with your sales efforts.

CHAPTER 2:
Determining the
Right Policy
For You

There's no right credit policy for every business. The best credit policy for you depends on your business, your customer, current economic conditions, the size of your bank account or company, how much credit you can afford to risk, and the likelihood you will get paid. In general, you should establish overall guidelines that are best suited to your current situation, then adapt them according to your assessment of the prospective debtor. We'll start with some basics and look more closely at how to assess your client, customer, or loanee later on in the book.

Various factors will affect whether you take a harder or more liberal line in each area--most notably, the general economic climate, the area where you do business, the nature of your business, your personal financial strength, the stability of your clientele (though you may vary your policy for different customers), and whether you emphasize expanding sales or reducing credit risks.

Hard Line or Soft Line?

A hard-nosed approach to credit usually emphasizes: taking cash or C.O.D. payments only; accepting checks only under limited circumstances (and requiring plenty of ID when you do); avoiding credit cards or checking them carefully; working up binding contracts; asking for large deposits; and getting payments in advance. This conservative approach may tend to restrict your sales, but you'll have more protection against poor credit risks--and in some situations, this is essential.

Conversely, with a more liberal policy, you'll: offer plenty of credit to qualified customers; take checks with only minimal ID; accept credit cards with a signature only; use informal contracts if any; and do work or ship products based only on a promise to pay. This will encourage new customers, but increase your likelihood of encountering payment problems.

Either approach, or something in between, can work for your business. As circumstances change, your approach can, too; always keep an eye on your current situation or market, and be ready to adjust policies if necessary.

General Economic Climate

When economic conditions are booming, you can afford to be more liberal with credit. You will be in a better financial position to extend it--and the people to whom you lend funds will be in a better position to pay. At the same time, when times are good, customers may be more demanding about expecting credit. If they know that other individuals and businesses are extending credit relatively freely, they will expect you to do so, too.

When times become difficult, extending credit becomes more risky. You may have financial problems yourself, and require more cash than usual to keep up with day-to-day expenses. You will face more risks, since individuals and companies may have more difficulty making payments. People are more likely to lose jobs or earn less pay; businesses are apt to have slow periods, and experience cash flow problems.

Adapt your policies to the times. In times of economic up- turn, be more willing to give credit; when things get tough, get tougher in offering credit.

Where You Live or Do Business

Where you live or do business is another crucial factor in how likely you are to get paid. In general, the higher the income level of the people who live in your neighborhood or patronize the area, the more comfortable you can feel about extending credit.

When you go shopping, you probably notice the difference ways credit is used. When you shop in a low income area, for example, all sales will usually be on a "cash up front" basis; merchants are unlikely to accept credit cards, and only a few will take checks. Some will have signs prominently located by the register: "All merchandise must be paid for in cash. NO EXCEPTIONS."

Some of these establishments even ask for payment in advance. Many self-service gas stations take this approach: you must go to the window before you can start pumping gas, pay what you estimate you will use, and then, if there's any change, go back to the window to get it. In some cases, you can still pay with a gasoline or all-purpose credit card-- but often this is not an option.

The rationale behind such a no-nonsense policy is clear enough: someone could easily fill up a tank and drive away. Moreover, if the customer fills up and can't pay--how do you take the gas back?

Given the high risks of doing business in a low-income area, it's no wonder most people want cash. On the other hand, as you move up the economic scale and look into stores in less depressed areas, you will see credit policies become more liberal. Small shops in working-class and lower-middle-class areas commonly don't accept credit cards, since few people in their area have cards and the merchants don't want to be bothered by the extra expense and hassle. But they will take checks with proper identification if drawn on local banks.

Moving further up the economic ladder, you'll find that stores in middle-income areas typically take credit cards and checks, though to protect themselves they frequently have a policy of calling a credit card clearing house or bank before approving the sale.

Finally, in more expensive and exclusive areas, credit cards become the name of the game. It's more or less expected that customers will pay for most purchases with a charge card, and very little checking is done. Usually, a signature is all that's necessary. The store owner assumes that if you buy the product or service, you have the ability and willingness to pay. Similarly, you'll find that checks much easier to cash in these areas--a quick look at a driver's license may be enough to complete the purchase.

Business owners may have special problems in dealing with people in wealthy areas. The rich are used to getting the finest products and services, and they can be very demanding, even finicky. Thus, a business catering to the wealthy can have more problems with returns, and more disputes over service, than other businesses. Such problems go with the territory; for better or worse, credit is the way the game is usually played.

As we have seen, then, the neighborhood where you do business will affect your risk of extending credit, and you'll find that certain general patterns of doing business have become established in the area. In this case, it's probably best to follow the crowd; an established business that has been around for a while has probably settled on a formula that works.

Once you're established, you can make your own minor adjustments. On the one hand, you may wish to increase your competitive sales advantage by offering slightly more liberal credit terms. Conversely, you can increase your protection against credit risks if you discover that other people in the neighborhood are frequently getting stuck. (To find out, simply go around, introduce yourself as a newcomer, and ask proprietors about their past experience in offering credit.)

The Nature of Your Business

The kind of business you are in will also influence your policies. Different businesses attract different types of customers; some are more stable and likely to pay than others. Your past history in dealing with credit questions should be taken into account. The size of your average transaction, and whether you expect to do business with the same customer or client more than once, will also come into play.

Be aware of what other individuals and companies in your field are doing. Suppose you are a small printer. It may be traditional for printers in your area to take 50 percent of the estimated cost of the job as a deposit and expect the rest on delivery. A doctor or lawyer might send a bill; a locksmith who goes out on a job normally gets a full payment with a check (or in cash) after completing the work. Unless you have a good reason for creating different credit and payment arrangements, it's probably to your benefit to look to others in your industry to set your general approach.

You might also be guided by the size of your transactions. If your sales are usually for small amounts, it may make more sense to get the full amount in cash, and perhaps selectively accept small checks. (Bear in mind, however, that if low-amount checks bounce, it's usually harder to collect than when a check is big enough to warrant calling the police or going to court.) If you have large sales, you are more likely to accept credit cards or checks (with appropriate credit checks, of course).

If your business lends itself to continuing client or customer contact, you can extend more credit than if it does not. At gas stations, for instance, most business is of the pass-through variety. The motorist stops by on his way to somewhere else; comparatively little business comes from residents of the area. This is why gas stations rarely accept checks. However, a corner drug store a few blocks away, which depends on regular customers, may take checks--and even skip checking IDs for most purchases, because the patrons are usually known to the staff personally.

As you continue to do business with the same customers, you can extend more credit. A printer I know starts off with 50 percent down and cash on delivery for everyone. After a few months, he takes small jobs with nothing down and bills on delivery with payment due in 30 days. For bigger jobs, the arrangement is 50 percent down and the rest due 30 days after billing.

In making credit decisions, keep your antennae attuned for changing conditions, even with a person you have learned to trust. You may have established a great relationship with a client or customer; perhaps you are used to receiving payment within seven days on all purchases when you obtain important new information. Maybe you sense his business is in trouble, or he has recently lost a job. Or perhaps the economy has grown soft. Take these developments into consideration. Perhaps you want to continue your current arrangement to give the person a break and help him get out of a hole. That's fine . . . if the signs point to good times ahead. If they don't, you may be setting yourself up to take a loss. Balance your compassion with an assessment of the cold, hard economic facts. Are you likely to win a continued customer by providing help in someone's time of need? Or does the situation seem terminal whatever you do? If so, you'll still lose your customer--and perhaps your own shirt, too.

Your Own Financial Strength

The amount of credit you can extend also depends on how strong you are financially. As you'll notice in looking closely at virtually any industry, the larger the company, the more likely it is to have credit arrangements. The bigger companies are better able to afford extended payments . . . and more likely to promote credit to make sales. In addition, some of the largest companies, like Sears and Macy's, offer their own credit cards!

These large companies, in turn, can better afford it when a customer defaults or is a slow pay, because they have huge customer bases, and can more easily work the cost of credit into the cost of other sales. If you're small and struggling, you don't have that luxury. A few wrong credit choices can put you under.

What all this means is that you have to base the credit you extend on your cash flow. If you need your income almost immediately to balance the books and stay afloat, it's probably better not to extend any credit. Just work on a cash-and-carry basis, perhaps permitting C.O.D.'s, checks, and a partial deposit down. As you get stronger, you can think about billing and credit cards, if your type of business and clientele warrant it.

The Overall Stability of Your Clientele

The two main factors to consider here are the economic power of your customers and the degree to which you expect repeat business. You can generally expect the profile of your customers to reflect the area where you do business. But that won't always be true.

For instance, some large businesses locate in a low-income or industrial area because the rents are low, but draw their customers from all over the city. This is the case with large lumber or household supply companies, who get retail customers not just from building contractors, but from customers at many points on the economic spectrum.

Analyze your customer base separately from the area where you do business; if you need to, start making notes when people come to buy or use your service. Who are these people? Try to establish their demographic profiles: sex; age; economic status; occupation or profession. Once you have learned who your customers are, you can fine-tune your financial policy accordingly.

For example, if your customers are primarily pre-teens or teenagers, as at some movie theaters or video arcades, then your arrangements should be strictly cash. By the same token, if your product or service appeals to people who are more likely to be on the move, like an auto repair shop, you will probably want to get cash or a credit card payment up front. (You may, in some cases, have some special options at your disposal--such as, in the auto repair business, a mechanic's lien on the car until you are paid. Even so, you usually want the money, not the car.)

On the other hand, if you have older customers, as the owner of a beauty parlor does, you know they'll tend to be more responsible about their debts, so checks are probably fine. Likewise, if you are dealing with solid, professional types, you are usually safe in taking checks or sending bills. (Consider the walk-in dentist in a shopping mall, who caters to the low-income customer with a dental emergency, and the dentist in a professional building who usually works with nearby office personnel. The dentist in the mall usually requires payment in advance; the other one is more likely to send his clients a bill.)

Expanding Sales Versus Reducing Credit Risks

Finally, consider how your credit policy is affecting sales. Is it interfering with sales in any way, and if so, how much? Would the increased profit from greater sales balance out the risk of losses from giving more credit?

To answer these questions, track your sales for a while, and try to determine whether you lose any sales because you won't extend credit. If you have a store in a mall or a booth in a trade show, make a note each time someone asks to make a purchase on a credit card and then doesn't buy because you don't offer that kind of credit. If only a few people ask and don't buy, you may not need this kind of service. Ask yourself whether people might walk by without stopping at all, because you don't prominently advertise that you offer credit. Monitor what the businesses around you do. If they take cards, perhaps you should too.

If you offer a service and your clients normally pay up at once, ask yourself if you have lost any clients because they would prefer to receive bills. Also consider the costs of offering credit. For example, at some banks that offer MasterCard or Visa, you have to pay the bank a minimum of $25 a month in discounts on sales (the percentage the bank deducts from each credit card sale you make when it pays you for the transaction). The only alternative is to make up the difference from your own account. If most of your customers aren't buying on credit, it may be costing you too much to keep the service.

Pay attention when callers seem concerned about your billing arrangements or decline your services when you say you expect payment by cash or check. If this happens, figure out your costs in lost clients versus possible losses if the clients you bill don't pay.

What are you likely to gain from extra sales?   What are you likely to lose from bad credit?   How much does the credit you offer really cost you?   Take into account the state of the economy, the area in which you live or do business, the nature of the your business, your own financial strength, and the type of clientele you are serving.

There's no exact formula for deciding--you have to assign your own rating system to evaluating the risks and gains. But the following chart can help you in making this assessment. Simply rate your strengths and weaknesses in each area to determine your likely losses and gains and note these on the chart. Then, add up the results and use these to help you decide: should you extend or restrict your credit? Or should you leave everything just as it is right now?

RISKS AND GAINS OF OFFERING CREDIT

(Using your best judgment, rate each of the following factors on their strengths and weaknesses. Use the following scale: from +5 – good risk – to -5 – bad risk. Then total up all the scores to arrive at your total credit assessment.)

Factors to be considered	Strengths **PLUS**	Not Sure **(0)**	Weaknesses **MINUS**
General economic climate			
Area where I live or do business			
Type of business			
Personal or business financial strength			
Stability of clientele			
My orientation toward expanding sales (PLUS) versus reducing credit risks (MINUS)			

Total:
Overall Risk or
Gain of Offering
Credit (add up the
MINUSES and
PLUSES)

CHAPTER 3:
Protecting
Yourself
Ahead of Time

To be in the best possible position to collect later if things go wrong, you have to do all you can to protect yourself in advance. This includes getting the proper identification so you can find the debtor or any assets later. In addition, you should also write up a good agreement or contract so you have an airtight claim on which to collect, and can pass your collection costs on to the debtor.

Taking a serious approach has several benefits. First, it puts your prospective customer, client, or loanee on notice that you are serious in expecting to be paid. You are less likely to attract debtors who think they can take advantage of you. Second, if you do have problems collecting later on, you will have a firm basis for reminding the debtor of his or her obligations--it's all down in black and white. Third, if you have to get tough by going to court or garnishing the debtor's assets, you have a better chance of tracking him and getting back your money, along with interest and costs.

Many people don't take such steps when they extend credit. They depend on oral agreements, or take personal checks on little more than faith.

That shouldn't be your credit approach. A few weeks or months later, when you realize you have a collection problem, you'll feel as though you're locking the barn after the horse is gone. All your efforts at that point may not be worth much; you may find the horse safely, all right--on the other side of a canyon.

The solution is to prepare yourself before the collection problem begins, so you can either avoid the problem altogether or be in a better position to confront it when it occurs. Just think of this as getting ready for a battle or plotting strategy in a war. Whether or not the battle or war actually happen, you want your weapons in order and the troops prepared.

When you look at collections this way, you're more likely to win. Think of the number of businesses that go bankrupt because of cash flow crises aggravated by bad debt. You don't want your business to fall into that category; accordingly, you must marshal all your resources and work to establish a strong credit policy.

Accepting Checks

Whenever you accept a check, you should not only review the check to make sure it is filled out properly, but also obtain a minimal amount of information about the person writing it. Of course, this will be unnecessary when a close friend, familiar and responsible customer, or associate is writing the check.

With people you don't know well or at all, however, you should do as most store owners do when you give them a check:confirm a few basics.

What to Check For

Typically, the kind of checking you should do involves making sure that the check is signed; that the correct amount is filled out in two places; that the "pay to the order of" line is made out to the right person or left blank so the payee can fill it in; that there's a preprinted address; and that there's a printed or written phone number. You should also ask to see a driver's license, and perhaps a major credit card, as identification, taking down appropriate numbers on the front of the check.

The logic behind such basic information requirements should be clear. For instance, if there's an address on the check, that's evidence that the person has had an account for at least a few weeks, which suggests at least a minimal degree of stability. The phone number allows you to call if there is any problem; if it's already printed on the check, so much the better. A driver's license reference is important, because the Department of Motor Vehicles is a key method of finding people (as drivers are supposed to keep their address current when they move or renew a license). If the person has a credit card, particularly one of the major ones, that's a further indication that you are dealing with an upstanding citizen: an applicant must survive some basic credit checks and have established a good credit record to get these cards.

Why You Should Take Extra Precautions

These preliminary checks are usually all you need for most situations involving small amounts, but if you're dealing with a person you don't know, are taking a relatively large check, or have any reason for concern, you can consider a few other protective steps. For example, if you are being written a big check, you might call the person's bank before you turn over the merchandise or perform a service for someone, just to be sure there's enough money in the account.

Be cautious; all sorts of strange things can happen after someone gives you a check. A check is only a promise to pay. You don't have the money until you have cash in hand.

What Can Go Wrong and How to Protect Yourself

Payment problems associated with personal checks can often be extremely difficult.

First, of course, a check can always be stopped. This is perfectly legal if the customer has a good reason to stop payment. If you have any reason to suspect this could happen--if, for instance, a customer has complained about high prices, or has talked about making returns if dissatisfied--you might wish to use some kind of agreement form as back-up, such as one stating that all claims for adjustment must be made within 15 days in writing. Later on, this will help you support your claims for payment if this is necessary.

Second, people who move--as about 20 percent of the U.S. population does each year--can easily continue to use old checks, and these often contain incorrect information. Therefore, you should confirm that the address on the check is still current and perhaps cross-check it against the address on the person's driver's license or other ID. When you do, be sure to ask if the driver's license or ID address is up-to-date. If the customer writes down a phone number, ask for both a day and evening number and see if you can get any other ID with one of those numbers for back-up. You might even ask for a business card as another safeguard.

Don't assume a person's identification is accurate. Even though it may look official, you're always better off verifying information and obtaining back-up identification wherever possible. This will minimize risks arising from both innocent mistakes and outright fraud.

With big checks, there is another potential danger: the possibility of insufficient funds, or a check drawn on an account that is (or soon will be) closed. People play all kinds of tricks with checks these days, and I know several people who have been burned. One apparently respectable travel promoter I encountered hired people to work for him, paid by check, then closed the account and opened another one in another bank. Checks that somehow snuck through this revolving-door arrangement tended to bounce. When people called to complain, the promoter's response was typical: "I'll send another check out today." The checks that followed (if, indeed, any were actually mailed at all) were as worthless as their predecessors.

Why You Can't Get Justice Right Away

One problem in dealing with checks that bounce is that you normally have very little legal clout to get your money back right away, even if the check writer is playing games and hasn't simply made an honest mistake. Furthermore, though your chances for winning are good, court cases can drag on interminably.

You don't have much power to demand immediate justice, because the police, as a general rule, don't bother with bad checks unless they are of a substantial amount. In Oakland, California, for instance, a bad check has to have been written for $150 or more, and issued within 90 days of the complaint, for the police to take any action. (There are some exceptions: the police may act on smaller checks if they are part of a pattern where the person is laying paper all over town.)

As a rule, police don't do much of anything on the smaller cases; if they did, they would be overwhelmed by the volume of bad checks written. In addition, law enforcement personnel often hesitate to act because, for criminal charges to be filed, the police must have grounds for believing the check writer had an intent not to pay at the time the check was written. This can be difficult to prove.

For example, let's assume a check bounces because the customer wrote checks for too much money in a one-week period. If there were funds in the account when the check was written, that suggests the customer could have had the intent to pay--even though you may believe he or she knowingly wrote too many checks. What's more, if the person wrote a check and closed the account the next day, there is still no strong proof of fraud, since the money was available when he or she wrote the check.

A bad check writer can always argue that he or she added the books wrong, or used the wrong checkbook, or expected someone to make a deposit. As you might imagine, there are any number of excuses.

Bad checks can be quite frustrating. You may be sure the check writer is making up a story; the police may even be sympathetic. But you won't be able to prove a thing. It's much better to take precautions earlier than to attempt to get justice after the fact.

Extra Precautions You Can Take

When you're uncertain about whether to take a check, there are a few things you can do in addition to collecting the usual information.

If you belong to a merchant's association or check-cashing service that collects the names of bad check writers, you can call up to verify whether the person is listed as a no-pay.

During banking hours, you can call the person's bank to verify an account's existence, and try to find out if there is enough money in it to cover the check. Simply call the bookkeeping department, say you are holding a check for a certain amount, give the name and account number, and ask if the check is good.

If you have doubts about whether the money will be in the bank in the morning or whether the person might stop the check, you might even consider visiting the bank in person to cash the check. Obviously, you can't hold every check to such standards; if you harbor doubts that are this serious, it's probably best not to take the check in the first place, though of course only you can be the judge of this.

If you get the check on an evening or weekend when you can't call the bank to verify, and you have any hesitations, you can decide to hold the merchandise until you have a chance to verify. Then you can either deliver it, or arrange for the customer to pick it up.

Waiting for Checks to Clear

An alternate strategy, if you are selling via mail order or expect payment in advance for your services, is to wait a week or two for the check to clear before you turn over any merchandise or engage in any work. If you use this approach, simply advise your customers or clients that if they pay by check, rather than by money order or certified funds, you will hold their merchandise or wait to do any work until the check clears. (Usually this is about five days for local checks, and ten to fifteen days on non-local or out-of-state accounts.) Code any mailing labels or work orders to reflect the date on which you deposited the check or the date on which you can freely ship or perform services. If the check comes back in the meantime, simply cancel the order and don't ship or do the work. (However, do send the customer a note. It's always possible he or she will send you another check or tell you to put the first check through again.)

This approach is particularly wise for out-of-town checks, for which everyday check verification is more time-consuming and follow-up on bad checks more difficult. Although most checks will be good, there is always the chance that you can run into problems with the bank.

Keeping Records of the Checks You Deposit

If you are accepting a check as a deposit and intend to bill for the balance, you might make a photocopy of the check; you won't see the check again unless it is no good. If you have any problems later in getting paid, and need to locate the customer's account, you will have a copy of the check with the account number, which is useful as long as the person keeps the same account. Also, any notations on the check, such as "payment on account" or "down payment, $500 balance due," will help bolster your case should it end up in court.

Another good way to protect yourself, though it will take a little longer, is to keep a check deposit record containing all important information from every check you deposit, including the person's name, address, phone number, bank account number, driver's license number, and any other credit data written on the check.

There are two major benefits in keeping this record. First, as with the photocopy method, you have a source of information you can use for follow-up if the check is a deposit or first payment, and the customer subsequently doesn't pay your bills. Moreover, if he or she gives you a bad check later and doesn't replace it with a good one, you have an additional (and potentially more reliable) source of information.

Second, you have a back-up record when you deposit your checks at your bank, in the unlikely event the bank loses your deposit. This will enable you to track down each check writer and get another check.

If you're going to take checks, then set up some "checks" in advance. Remember, you don't have the money until it's in the bank.

CHAPTER 4:
Maximizing Your Personal Security

This chapter will deal with the options available to you that will maximize your chances of collecting on a given debt if there are payment problems. We will take a close look here at contracts, promissory notes, and collateral.

Contracts and Promissory Notes

To avoid the problems of oral agreements, write the understanding down--either in the form of a promissory note stating how much is owed (and when), or in a contract outlining the specific terms of your agreement.

Getting a Promissory Note

Whenever you extend credit, you can use a promissory note detailing the money owed, when any payments will be made, and when the entire balance comes due. The promissory note also indicates any money paid in advance, the amount loaned or financed, any finance charges, and the terms of payment (how much is payable, how often, starting when, and the grand total).

A note commonly states, too, that if a payment is missed, the creditor may demand the whole balance--and that if the creditor accepts a late payment, the remaining balance is still due. It may further include a small late charge (say five to twenty-five dollars, depending on the size of the loan), and it may state that the debtor is responsible for paying any costs of collection and attorney's fees. It is signed by both lender and debtor.

Following is a representative note used by a loan company. You can create your own, and perhaps write a less formal one for dealings with a business associate or friend. But be sure to include all the elements noted above.

PROMISSORY NOTE

Amount of Note: $ _____ Date: _____

For value received, the undersigned promise(s) to pay to the order of
the sum of (1) $ (amount of note) as follows:

paid herewith (2) $ (down payment)

leaving a balance of (3) $ (total financed)

plus finance charge of (4) $ (finance charge)

for a total of payments of (5) $ (total you will pay)

The annual percentage rate is 12 per cent simple interest.

TERMS OF PAYMENT: $ payable on   /   /   , and
$ each   thereafter, beginning on   /   /   , with a final
installment of $ for a total of   payments.

DEFAULT in the payment of any installment shall, at the option of, and without notice or demand, render the entire balance at once due and payable. Acceptance of any late payment shall not constitute a waiver of any subsequent payment when due.

IF SUIT is instituted to collect on this note, the undersigned promise(s) and agree(s) to pay the cost of such action, together with attorney fees in such amount as may be fixed by the court.

CONSIDERATION for this promissory note is: Forbearance of legal action in the matter of: vs.   .

Signer: Co-Signer:

x   x

print names:

address:

this note signed at:

(city)   (state)

on this date:

we received a copy of this note:

(initial)   (initial)

Besides using a promissory note to firm up your initial agreement to extend credit, you can seek one later on, as will be discussed, to reaffirm a debt where there is a verbal agreement or any possibility of dispute.

Writing Effective Contracts

Regardless of the specifics of your financial policies, contracts are useful for clarifying your agreements--and giving you documentation should you have to go to court. Although   verbal contracts are valid, and some people pride themselves on working on trust, a good written contract will spell out what is agreed more accurately and precisely.

Advantages of a Written Contract

An effectively written contract does two things. It makes clear what services or products you are offering in return for a given payment. It also serves as proof of what the other party has agreed to in collection settings--and, if necessary, in court.

The problem with verbal agreements is that people often have different understandings or different memories about what was agreed. When a dispute develops, it can be difficult to prove what a contract contained--or even whether it existed in the first place. A written contract, on the other hand, is solid proof of the agreement.

What to Include in a Contract

When you write a contract about a sale, loan, work project,   or other creditor/debtor arrangement, the contract should always contain the following information:

A description of the service or loan.

The amount of payment expected, and when due.   (If there are installments,   the contract can indicate the penalties if a payment is missed--such as   interest on the balance or an option for the creditor to demand the entire   amount.)

The length of time the agreement will last, if ongoing transactions are   involved (such as when you hire a consultant on a monthly retainer.)

Under what circumstances, if any, the contract may be terminated and by   whom.

How the customer or client might act if he/she has any complaint about the   product or service.   (For example, a contract might indicate that a   customer has up to 30 days to return the merchandise for a full refund,   or for a refund less a 10 percent service charge; otherwise, it is assumed   the customer has received the merchandise in satisfactory condition.)

What recourse the creditor has if the customer or client fails to pay, such as the ability to collect interest, collection costs, attorney's fees,   court costs, and other expenses.

Say What You Mean

Many informal agreements fail to go into enough detail. The customer or client might have one interpretation, the creditor another, and (should the case go to court) the judge still another.

For example, I once introduced a casual acquaintance, Jack, to a business associate, Paul. Paul thought he was going to make a fortune in a new business based on recruiting a network of people who wanted to join a savings club. He was looking for people to lend him money so he could promote the club, with the agreement that he would also pay back 25 percent on the principal and put them in the business, too. Unfortunately, the whole venture went under. It was when my acquaintance tried to collect on his loan, and couldn't, that my contract problems began.

This occurred because I had written up an agreement acknowledging responsibility for making the introduction. In return, I agreed to do everything I could to see that Jack was repaid. Now according to federal and California law, a person does not take on the financial obligation of another person or become a guarantor for a loan to someone else, without agreeing to do so in writing. I had also informed   the creditor verbally when we wrote up the agreement that I was not in a position to assume liability for the loan itself. But we didn't specifically state in the contract that I didn't have this obligation.

When Jack took Paul to court, the contract was sufficiently ambiguous for Jack to seek to include me as a defendant too. If he couldn't collect from Paul, he claimed to be able to do so from me. Legally he couldn't, since I didn't agree to assume liability in the contract. But because of the vague statement concerning assuming responsibility for the introduction, there was enough in our memo of agreement to create a time-consuming obligation for me. As my lawyer explained the dilemma, "He has enough to take you into court, but not enough to win." This turned out to be completely accurate.

To avoid such problems, clarify your contract so that everyone involved--you, the debtor, and, just as important, someone not a party to your agreement--can understand exactly what has been negotiated.

Insert a Collection Costs Clause in Your Contracts

Many unscrupulous debtors assume creditors will give up efforts to collect because of the high cost involved. Disappoint them. Include a clause in any contract or loan agreement stating that the debtor will be responsible for the costs of collection if the debt isn't paid when due. This way, you can get back reasonable collection expenses and interest. Without such a clause, you usually can't charge overdue interest or add on your collection expenses, except for those incurred as court costs.

The clause might read something like this: "If the amount due in this agreement is not paid by the date indicated, and it is necessary to take steps to collect on this debt, then the client (customer, loanee) agrees to pay all reasonable collection costs, including attorney fees, that are necessary to collect the debt."

The following is a good example of a protection clause used by a consulting company. This firm requires a client to commit to a business development program with a monthly retainer for at least three months, and requires a 90-day termination notice. It specifies in straightforward terms the client's obligations to pay:

> In the event Client terminates this Agreement and fails to make payments as specified in this Agreement, Client shall, in addition to the aforementioned payments [the monthly retainer fee], be liable for the costs associated with [the company's] attempts to collect said payments including, but not limited to, attorney's fees, court costs, collection costs and any and all miscellaneous expenses, and shall make reimbursement of said costs and expenses to [the company] seven (7) days from the date upon which [the company] provides Client with documentation of same.

Now that kind of statement shows the creditor is really serious. You don't want to mess with someone who has a contract like that!

Should your prospective customer or client raise any objections to this clause, you can downplay its significance in the interests of good will. For example, you might say something like,   "Oh, that's just a routine clause our accountant requires us to have on every agreement," or "I'm sure you don't have to worry about that, since you'll be paying us on time. That's just to protect us if there is any problem in collecting."

If the person continues to resist signing, that's a signal that you may have some problems down the road. Maybe he or she has some doubts about being able to pay, or has a pattern of getting into disputes about the bill. Be careful.

Making Sure Your Client/Customer Understands the Contract

Once you have an airtight contract, be sure your customer or client reads it so that everything is completely understood and there are no recriminations later. Where appropriate, read the document over with your customer or client on the spot; answer any questions that come up.

On the other hand, if a careful on-the-spot reading and signing won't work for you, another approach might be to invite your client/customer to take a contract form home to review, and then finalize things at another meeting. Alternatively, you might go over the major points in the contract, explain that this is your standard policy, and ask your client or customer to read the contract in detail, and sign and return it within the next three days. Then he or she can call if necessary to discuss questions or problems.

In brief, balance your enthusiasm to make a sale with your need to get a signed contract that your customer or client can can freely accept and pay on the terms agreed.

Getting a Commitment

Finally, if appropriate, get a down payment as a show of commitment, even if you have to take a postdated check for a contract that won't go into effect for several months. A deposit shows you the signer is serious--and indicates that you are, too. If you are setting up a retainer arrangement for a month or two hence, you might ask for part of the amount on signing to "hold the space" or "reserve the commitment."

Collateral

When you are extending only a small amount of credit, it may not make sense to ask for collateral. But as the monetary stakes increase, getting some security for your credit makes more and more sense. If the debtor doesn't pay up, you get the collateral. If he or she declares bankruptcy, you are have a degree of protection, because the secured creditors are paid off first. If you have rights to that collateral free and clear, you will get it all.

Making the Arrangements

All sorts of things can be considered collateral: objects, rights to property, accounts receivable, cars, furniture, even merchandise in a store. Sometimes a debtor will say he doesn't have anything to put up for collateral, but has not considered all the assets in question.

To get collateral, you have to ask for it, since the debtor isn't likely to volunteer it. However, when you ask, most people will go along with your offer, particularly if you present it correctly.

First, make your request sound like your regular policy; if you are dealing with a friend or business associate who might be miffed at the implication you don't trust him or her, you can, as usual, blame it on your accountant. ("Yeah, I know we don't really need it in your case-- but our accountant has told us to do it, so that's our policy.")

Second, make the debtor see that it is to his or her advantage to make this arrangement. Point out that since you have collateral, you can extend more credit or extend it for a longer time. If you're in a competitive selling situation, you can explain that this collateral enables you to give the person better terms than he or she might get from someone else: you can be more liberal because you've got the collateral for security.

Making Sure Your Collateral Protects You

One possible problem with collateral occurs when a person uses the same item or items as collateral with more than one creditor. Another difficulty can arise if the person specifies the order in which collateral holders get to exercise their right, and you find after a sale of the collateral that there isn't enough left for you. Then, too, if the person isn't honest, he or she may sell off your collateral without informing you, rendering your attempts to collect on it moot.

Verify that the collateral in question is pledged only to you, or that your rights in a shared item or set of items are clearly specified. That way, you will know whether there's enough collateral to satisfy your interests. (You might also check up from time to time to make sure your collateral is still on hand.)

Make sure the amount of collateral you receive is equal to the amount of credit you offer. Don't accept collateral that's worth less than the debt--if you do, the debtor may have less incentive to pay the whole amount.

Set up a repayment agreement if you expect the debtor to pay you back over time. In this agreement, indicate that the payments must be made when due . . . and that if they are not made when due, you have the right to require payment of the entire amount--or take your collateral at that time if payment is not made.

Ascertain that the collateral is really worth what you think it is. To do this, assume that you will have to sell the collateral yourself either directly or at an auction; estimate what this sale value would be. (Remember, this sale value can vary tremendously depending on the circumstances.)

Find out if there are other claims against the asset (for example, learn whether another creditor has already placed a lien on a car, or whether there is an existing mortgage on a house). Subtract the value of these claims to determine what you have left. You can get a general idea about other claims by asking your customer or client. However, if a sizable amount is involved, it's worth doing some extra checking to be sure. Some people aren't totally honest, or they forget. You can check various public records, such as the Department of Motor Vehicles to find out about a lien on a car or the Tax Assessor's Office to find out about any liens on a house.

Write up a clear and effective security agreement to protect your collateral. The agreement should incorporate these elements:

(1) Date, name and address of the debtor, and name of the creditor.

(2) A statement about what is pledged.

(3) A statement that the security will include similar property the debtor acquires. (For example, if a debtor has put up some tools as security and trades them in for a better set of tools, the new tools become part of your collateral.)

(4) A statement that the collateral will be kept at the debtor's address and will be adequately insured, if the creditor re- quests this.

(5) A statement that the debtor owns the collateral free and clear and so is able to pledge it as security.

(6) A statement that if the debtor defaults on any payment or otherwise breaches this agreement, the creditor can declare the whole balance due.

(7) A clause indicating that the debtor will be responsible for any reasonable costs of collections and attorneys' fees in the event of a default or breach of contract.

(8) The signature of the debtor and creditor.

For an even stronger security agreement, you can add a clause stating that the value of the collateral must at least remain at the value of the debt. This way, if you work out an agreement giving you some general category of property as security (such as inventory on hand or the debtor's accounts receivable) which had a certain value when you signed the agreement, the debtor can't start selling off part of this property to reduce it below the value of your security. If so, you can immediately demand your cash.

Another strategy is to include a comprehensive clause that expands your collateral to include other assets if the collateral originally pledged isn't enough to satisfy your debt. For example, don't just ask for inventory as security; ask in addition for other assets that the business or individual owns. Then if there are problems later, you have more leverage to collect.

Continue to monitor the amount of collateral on hand. Don't just take your debtor's word for it. If the individual or business doesn't pay, the debtor may be having many other financial problems, too, and might start selling off inventory or assets that represent your collateral. If your collateral includes receivables, ask for a list of these every few months to make sure you are still protected.

If you decide to extend more credit, write up another security agreement--or add a clause to your first one stating that your collateral balance is increased to cover the new debt. Alternatively, if you are going to be extending credit on an ongoing basis, include a clause stating that collateral worth the value of the debt will be applied to cover both present and future debts.

Obtaining Co-Signers

You may want to make a loan or close a sale, but be unsure about the prospective debtor's ability to handle the obligation. That's the time to suggest that the individual consider getting a co-signer or guarantor.

One situation where you might well want to do this is when someone is just starting a business and seems obviously undercapitalized. With some credit, the venture might make it. To reduce your risk, you might ask the new owner to get a co-signer, such as a relative, business associate, or close friend. Similarly, if someone who doesn't have much of a credit history wants a loan, you might offer to make the loan if someone else will guarantee it.

Another common situation where a co-signer might be advisable is where extending credit to a small company set up as a corporation may seem too risky. In this case, ask the owner or key officers or stockholders to guarantee personally any credit or loan. (If the company is a partnership or proprietorship, you don't need a special agreement, since the owners are automatically liable.)

If you do get a guarantor or co-signer, check his or her credit as carefully as you would the original signer, because if you have any problems collecting from the signer, you'll have to collect from the guarantor.

Since an individual is not legally liable for another person's debt unless he or she specifically assumes the debt in writing, you should draw up a firm guarantee or co-signer agreement. Specifically, the guarantee agreement should state that:

The guarantor understands he or she has an absolute and unconditional responsibility to pay and cannot make any counterclaims against the creditor.

The guarantor agrees to cover any and all debts due from the debtor, including any interest or other charges. (If you expect an ongoing credit relationship, try to get the guarantor to agree both to debts that are due now and those that the debtor makes subsequently. You can also limit the guarantee to a specific debt and limit the credit you extend accordingly.)

The guarantor agrees to remain bound by the agreement even if the terms are changed or extended in some way or if another guarantor or party to the loan is released from the agreement. (The guarantor should also agree to remain bound if there should be any substitution in the collateral used to secure the loan.)

The guarantor understands that he or she is assuming primary liability; if there are two or more guarantors, they understand they are assuming joint and primary liability. (If you don't state this, you have to do everything you can to collect from the original debtor first--and whether you have done your best can be open to much interpretation.)

The guarantor agrees that there is no time limit on how long his guarantee lasts; rather, it will continue as long as the debt does.

The guarantor agrees to pay all collection costs and attorney fees necessary to collect on this agreement.

Will the guarantor go along with this kind of ironclad contract? Some may, some may not; you may lose some deals. But that may be all for the best. After all, if you aren't sure about extending credit in the first place, you don't want to end up with a guarantee arrangement that isn't going to give you complete security.

Conditional Sales, Consignment, and Inventory as Security

If you are in the business of selling a product, there are several creative ways to promote your business and protect yourself, too. These include making a conditional sale, selling your merchandise on consignment, or releasing your inventory to the buyer on a gradual basis until the buyer pays for all of it.

Conditional Sales

If the debtor wants to buy something you own but can't pay in full, you can protect yourself through a conditional sale. This way, you still have title to the item until the debtor pays you in full; if he or she doesn't pay, you take it back. The customer only gets title after paying in full.

This approach is ideal for larger, more expensive items, like a boat or car. You transfer the registration to the debtor when you make the sale but keep the title until he or she pays.

When you make a conditional sale agreement, there are a number of points your agreement should include. First, of course, the text must make it clear that this is a conditional sale in which the seller retains full title to the goods until they have been paid for in full. The agreement should also specify: the items being sold; the basic price and any additional charges, such as sales tax, finance charge, and insurance; the amount paid down and any other credits; the balance for which the seller is extending credit and any interest charged on this; and the amount of payment expected each week or month and when this payment starts.

Furthermore, the agreement should include consent by the buyer that he or she will keep the goods safely at the address indicated on the agreement, and will not permit any other liens to be put upon them. You should also attach a   statement that the full balance will be due if the debtor defaults and that the debtor will pay any reasonable costs of collection and attorney fees. In addition, the seller can take the goods back and sell them to secure payment, adding on any expenses to the amount due. Finally, your agreement should include the name, address and signature of both the buyer and the seller.

Consignments

Another effective approach, one that some manufacturers and publishers use to extend credit to retailers, is that of selling on consignment. In some cases sellers use a formal consignment agreement, which states that the retailer has received the items in good condition; will display them and use his or her best efforts to sell them; will give the seller an accounting within a certain period after the sale; and will return the items on demand if unsold. Generally, though, consignment arrangements are relatively informal when small amounts of merchandise are involved, such as when less than one hundred books are placed on on consignment in a chain of area bookstores.

In such an informal arrangement, the merchant makes an

inventory of the items on a letterhead or purchase order, indicates the commission or discount from the retail sales price, notes the final date for the seller to pick up the items not sold, signs it, and gives a copy to the seller. The seller then checks back periodically to see if the merchant needs more stock, or arranges to pick up the items that do not move.

If you can, get the merchant to assume responsibility for any damages, so that if your merchandise is damaged while on consignment, you have an understanding of what you are entitled to collect. Otherwise you may experience what happens to many sellers when they get back damaged merchandise: the merchant tries to escape any responsibility with a comment like, "Well, I did what I could to sell it, but that's what happens when something is on the shelf for awhile."

When you do consignment selling, you are extending credit and you should get the same sort of protection any creditor gets. Too often small business people feel so thankful to get any display space at all that they fail to see that they are taking most of the risk and should at least have the credit they are extending firmly secured.

Ask for an agreement. Explain that it's your usual policy and point out that it's to the merchant's advantage, because with the agreement in place you'll see that he or she has a continuous supply of goods. Present the credit you are offering as something of value, and the merchant will be more receptive to your request for security.

Using Inventory as Security

If you are doing business with someone who is short of cash, needs the products or services you offer, and seems honest and likely to succeed, you can use your inventory or the work you do as security. Under this arrangement, the person gives you an order for what he or she needs, but you only deliver a small part of it at intervals. The customer or client pays you on each delivery, or as you complete another phase of the work. It's a calculated risk that the debtor will stay in business--and if it works, you'll probably not only get paid but end up with a long-term mutually beneficial business relationship, too.

Joe did this very successfully in his electronics parts business. Paul, who started a small manufacturing company, wanted about $20,000 worth of parts over a year, and Joe could supply those parts. Since Paul wasn't in a strong financial position, Joe wouldn't give him credit for the whole thing. Instead, he shipped about 20 percent of the order at a time. After Paul paid for that, Joe shipped another 20 percent. In effect, he extended about $4,000 in credit--but in return, gained a $20,000 order. At the same time, he persuaded Paul to put up some equipment worth about $4,000 as security. Eventually he got all his money, and they continued to do business together.

What made this arrangement work so well was that Joe had a product Paul desperately wanted and couldn't easily get from someone else. As a result, Paul was essentially locked into dealing with Joe and paying him back. So Joe could cut a tougher deal: he had something Paul wanted and could get only from him.

CHAPTER 5:
Extending
Commercial Credit

While many consumer purchases are made on a "cash only" basis, businesses must often extend credit when selling to other businesses. This is the norm in most industries; even offers of added discounts for prepayment are, as a rule, met with little enthusiasm by purchasing firms. At the same time, there are some industries in which advance payment or payment upon delivery is the norm. If you can avoid extending credit, by all means do so. Determine what the prevailing standards are in your industry and in your local region.

Even if the norm in your industry is to extend credit, you will not want to extend credit automatically to all who ask for it. You must establish a policy once you determine who your best credit risks are. If you conclude that you should not extend credit to a certain business, then don't! Either try to obtain full payment in advance or, failing that, partial payment. (Depending on your business environment, you may also wish to consider accepting a deposit, with full payment on receipt of the product or service.) Walk away from the sale if you cannot obtain the terms you feel are appropriate. This may seem like a drastic course, but for many smaller businesses it only takes one or two large bad debts to take the entire business under.

Simple Credit Criteria

Though you may be extending credit for a relatively small amount to other businesses (say from $100 to $500), take the time and energy to learn about credit history wherever possible. Check first to see how the firm pays its bills--before you check a company's income statement (the opposite of the approach to consumer credit checks). Income for businesses is much more erratic than for individuals. Even if the business was very profitable for the last three years, it might have lost a major customer recently, or be in the midst of serious financial problems for other reasons. Even a very profitable business may sometimes fail to pay its bills due to cash flow problems. For example, when fast growth requires a firm to carry much larger inventories and much higher levels of receivables, payments can slip.

Ask for the names of other vendors, bearing in mind that a firm is likely to give you the names of vendors paid in a timely manner. If possible, obtain the names of three to six vendors. You may not need to call

all of them, but at least you will have that option.

Try to get references that provide approximately the same type of service or goods as your firm would, and are roughly the same size. The fact that a grocery store pays bills promptly for food vendors is no guarantee that it will pay an advertising bill quickly. A retailer is much more likely to pay its merchandise vendors on time than its service vendors because it is extremely dependent on the former group for day-to-day business operations. By the same token, if you are a small vendor selling one small product to a retailer, you cannot expect to be paid as quickly as the largest wholesalers or manufacturers.

In your contacts with credit references, be sure to ask how long it usually takes the firm in question to pay its bills. Find out the total amount of credit extended now, and how long the current balance has been outstanding. You should also determine the largest amount of credit extended to date, as well as the length of time that credit has been extended. In addition, you might want to ask what the firm's maximum credit line is, and how promptly it has made payments, particularly in recent months.

Exercise some judgment in evaluating this basic credit information. Even if the firm is current with all its references, you might still decide not to extend any credit--if, for example, you discover that the firm has often been late with payments, or if it appears to have exhausted maximum credit lines at each of its vendors.

When you evaluate a firm's payment history, compare its payment history to the industry standard (as opposed to the terms on the invoice). In many industries, for example, the industry standard is to pay invoices only at 60 days or even later, even if the invoice states "net 30." Realistically speaking, you cannot expect to be paid before the industry average, especially if you are a new or small business. But you can certainly try to get paid as soon as possible.

Some firms give out as "credit" references the names of vendors with whom they have just started doing business, and to whom they have not yet made a single payment. If this happens to you, recognize that these are not credit references at all, and ask for real references. If the firm will offer only meaningless referrals, you will have a good indication that you should insist on payment in advance. It is quite likely that the firm's credit history is unsatisfactory.

How Much Credit?

Once you decide to extend credit to a firm, the next question is quite straightforward: how much? If you are at all hesitant about your decision, start out with a very small credit line. You can always increase the credit line later. And if you ship fewer goods initially, the firm may well return for a re-order sooner, giving you more leverage toward payment for the first order. Unfortunately, you will find that some companies will not pay you until they need your goods or services again. This may even occur when dealing with prestigious or well-established firms.

Do not be afraid to deny or limit credit to a very large firm. The largest corporations in the world can go bankrupt. Even assuming that the organization remains solvent, it is often quite difficult to collect a small bill from a huge firm. If you are not a regular vendor, you might find yourself calling one department after another trying to track down any number of people involved in completing the necessary paperwork.

(Note: Whenever you sell on credit, you should get a written purchase order--and a written receipt if you deliver a product. If the order is placed over the phone and the company resists taking the time to mail a purchase order, ask to have a copy of the purchase order faxed to you. The receipt is even more important; larger companies in particular can be difficult if not impossible to collect from without a written receipt.)

With regard to the smaller amounts of credit (less than $500), checking with two or three appropriate current vendors is usually sufficient.

The Bank Reference

For a decision that involves a significant amount of money (over $500) more work is in order. In this case, the next step is to ask for bank references. Call the bank's accounting department and ask for the account balance. (The bank will probably release only very rough average balance information.) Ask how long the account has been open. If the bank won't release such information, you may be out of options. Some businesspeople, facing this problem, will call the bank and state that they have a check for X dollars from the company in question, and want to know whether it will clear (often, several calls are necessary over a period of days to get an idea of the balance).

Of course, if the applicant can give a personal reference at a bank, this can be very helpful. Explain to the reference why you are calling, then ask for as much information as possible. Ask:

How long have you known the applicant?

Does the business have a line of credit at your bank?

Has the business ever borrowed funds before?

Has the business always paid back borrowings on time?

How much does the business owe now?

What is the most the business has ever owed?

How does the business seems to be performing now?

Checking Credit References

Many businesses rely very heavily on credit rating services such as Dun & Bradstreet and TRW. You may want to consider using these services, especially before extending larger amounts of credit. These firms will provide important facts such as a history of the firm, abbreviated financial data, ownership information, and some credit payment records.

As a general rule, you should place more weight on information from the major credit rating services for larger firms than for smaller ones; reports on the larger firms tend to be more carefully researched, while financial information about smaller firms is often obtained directly from the principal of the firm, without outside verification. In addition, the rating service will usually only check the payment history of a very small number of vendors for these firms. Then, too, it may check only those vendors the company suggests.

Sharing Credit Information

Another way to get accurate and up-to-date credit information is to share credit information with other firms working in the same industry as you. The biggest advantage to this approach is that you do not have to rely so strongly on the references that the credit applicant chooses to provide.

There may be an association of credit managers in your industry; if so, consider joining. Alternatively, you might want to set up your own group, or at least develop informal relationships with a few credit managers at other firms serving the same industry.

Evaluating Financials

While a firm's recent and current payment history is generally the best indicator of whether or not you will be paid on a timely basis, you should also consider evaluating financial statements, particularly if a large amount of credit is requested. Financial statements can provide a good indication of the firm's ability to pay debts over the short and long term.

Following are income statements and balance sheets you can ask the applicant to fill out. The applicant may even provide you with previously completed financial statements. Have an officer of the applicant's firm sign the financials, particularly if the statements are not prepared and signed by a certified public accountant (CPA).

BALANCE SHEET
INDIVIDUAL/PARTNERSHIP

ASSETS

Cash:	_____
Accounts receivable:	_____
Less bad debt allowance:	_____
Inventory:	_____
Loan to partners, key employees:	_____
Depreciable, depletable and intangible assets:	_____
Less accumulated depreciations, depletion and amortization:	_____
Real estate:	_____
Other assets:	_____
TOTAL ASSETS	_____

LIABILITIES

Accounts payable:	_____
Taxes:	_____
Other current liabilities:	_____
Loans:	_____
Mortgages, notes, bonds payable:	_____
Net worth:	_____
TOTAL LIABILITIES	_____

Signed: _____ Date: _____

PROFIT & LOSS STATEMENT

Year: _____

INCOME

Gross sales: _____

Less returns: _____

Less bad debt: _____

Interest, rent, royalty income: _____

TOTAL INCOME _____

EXPENSES

Cost of goods sold: _____

Direct payroll: _____

Indirect payroll: _____

Taxes, other than income tax: _____

Sales expenses: _____

Shipping, postage: _____

Advertising, promotion: _____

Office expenses: _____

Travel, entertainment: _____

Phone: _____

Other utilities: _____

Auto/truck: _____

Insurance: _____

Professional fees: _____

Rent: _____

Interest on loans: _____

Other: _____

TOTAL EXPENSE BEFORE TAX _____

NET INCOME _____

INCOME TAX _____

NET INCOME AFTER TAX _____

Signed: _____ Date: _____

CORPORATE BALANCE SHEET

ASSETS

Cash: _____

Accounts receivable: _____

Less bad debt allowance: _____

Inventory: _____

Loan to stockholders: _____

Depreciable, depletable
and intangible assets: _____

Less accumulated depreciations,
depletion and amortization: _____

Other assets: _____

TOTAL ASSETS _____

LIABILITIES

Accounts payable: _____

Taxes: _____

Other current liabilities: _____

Loans from stockholders: _____

Mortgages, notes, bonds payable: _____

Other liabilities: _____

Capital Stock: _____

Paid-in or capital surplus: _____

Retained earnings: _____

Less cost of treasury stocks: _____

**TOTAL LIABILITIES
AND STOCKHOLDER'S EQUITY** _____

Signed: _____ Date: _____

The most important question about the financials is not really about profits, size, or net worth, as might be expected. Rather, the key question is: who filled out the financials? Knowing the answer will help you assess how accurate and complete the forms are.

Were the forms you are examining filled out by the applicant? An outside bookkeeper? A CPA? Statements prepared by CPAs are worthy of much more credibility than virtually any others.

Of course, even if a CPA did assemble the financials, this does not tell you who really produced the original numbers. To gain any insight into this question, you should be aware of how this data is customarily assembled.

Basically, there are three levels of financial statements: the compilation, the review, and the audit.

In preparing a compilation, the CPA takes the numbers provided by the client and arranges them into financial statements without any analysis or verification.

In preparing a review, the CPA will, in addition to compiling the financial statements, perform some review of the analytical process from which the numbers were created, but engage in only minimal verification. At the compilation or review level, the CPA does not express an opinion as to the accuracy or soundness of the financial statements taken as a whole.

The best financial statements are audited, meaning that the CPA has not only compiled and reviewed the financial statements, but has also done some verification of the information provided by the company. Furthermore, the CPA will express an opinion with regard to the financial statements and assume significant liability for their accuracy.

To be sure, there are many instances of fraud that even the largest and most prestigious accounting firms are unable to detect when examining financial statements. Nonetheless, an audited financial statement with a favorable accountant's opinion is usually a sign of a sound financial structure; the information is generally quite reliable. Unfortunately, for very small firms the cost of obtaining audited financial statements is prohibitive. As a result, you cannot expect audited financials from the smallest companies.

Do be sure to determine when the documents were assembled. If the statements were prepared ten months ago, and the business has only existed for three years, chances are the current financial situation is quite different by now. You might want to ask for interim financial statements, or perhaps for additional information about a few key items (such as accounts receivable, inventory, loan balances and cash).

The Balance Sheet

In contrast to the methods used in evaluating an individual for credit, when evaluating the creditworthiness of a business it is a good idea to give more emphasis to the balance sheet than the income statement. Even if a business is profitable, it will not always be able to pay its bills on a timely basis if it is severely undercapitalized or simply runs out of cash temporarily.

First look at the firm's cash position. If the company has little cash, no other liquid assets, and no bank credit, it probably is not paying its bills on time now. It will probably not pay you on time either.

Next, look at the firm's working capital ratio. The working capital ratio is the firm's current assets (primarily cash, accounts receivable, inventory and prepaid expenses) divided by the current liabilities (liabilities due within one year, such as short-term loans, accounts payable, accrued payroll, accrued taxes, and so on). If the ratio of current assets to current liabilities is less than one to one, the firm is almost certainly facing a liquidity crisis and is a poor credit risk. On the other hand, if the working capital ratio is greater than two, the firm is probably an excellent credit risk. Even a current ratio of 1.5:1 is generally considered acceptable. When the ratio falls to between 1.5:1 and 1:1, be more cautious. Carefully weigh all other considerations before deciding to extend credit.

In addition, look at the ratio of the company's total debt to total equity. While some Fortune 500 firms might survive with a very high debt ratio, a total debt to equity relationship of greater than 1:1 generally reflects instability in a smaller firm. Read the footnotes carefully on financial statements and beware of off-the-balance sheet financial commitments (such as real estate or equipment leases).

By comparing the payables total on the balance sheet and the expense figures from the income statement, you should be able to make an educated guess at the average aging of the company's payables. Take the company's total expenses (less any expenses that were prepaid) and divide by the payables outstanding on the balance sheet; then multiply by 365 days. This will give you, roughly, the number of days it takes the company to pay its average bill. However, if the business is seasonal or rapidly growing, this number will have little significance. Remember that your firm is not necessarily going to be paid when the average bill is paid--especially if you are a new vendor, or if your bill arrives at a time of high growth or increased seasonal activity.

The Income Statement

While the income statement is less useful than the balance sheet for evaluating credit risks when selling to other businesses, you should still examine it. Pay more attention to the percentage of profitability in comparison to sales than to the total profits.

Ask yourself: is the company profitable enough to survive and to make it worthwhile for the owner to continue in business? Is the profit margin large enough to sustain a slight increase in expenses or a slight decrease in sales?

If the business is incorporated, another critical figure to look for is whether or not the owners pay themselves salaries. If the profitability of the firm appears small, but the owners take out large salaries, then the firm could actually be performing quite well. (Alternatively, the owners could be taking too much from the company, leaving it in a weakened cash flow position.) In this low-profits, high salaries situation, you might want to consider asking the owners to guarantee their credit line personally--particularly if the firm has few assets.

Is the profit margin distorted by a lot of non-cash expenses, such as depreciation? Perhaps the business shows a heavy depreciation charge for real estate, even though the value of the real estate in the area is actually appreciating each year!

If you can, note important trends by comparing financial statements from more than one year. Are fast-growing sales leaving the company with a deteriorating working capital ratio? Is debt increasing? Is the profit margin declining?

Making the Credit Decision

While many decisions about when to extend credit will be clear-cut, there will be situations where the firm's credit worthiness appears to fall into the borderline category. Be wary of extending credit in these situations simply because the person seems to have a solid character; solid character alone does not pay the bills. In any case, you should not hesitate to deny credit if you have an uneasy feeling about the character of the businessperson you are evaluating. When you feel distrust, it's usually good to go with your gut feelings.

Alternatively, you may be able to develop a "borderline solution" for hard-to-settle credit questions. For example, if you can't decide whether or not to approve a requested $1,000 credit line for a new customer, consider starting with $500. Another common alternative is to require that the first order be prepaid, in full or in part, or cash on delivery.

Pay particularly close attention to whether your "borderline" cases adhere to your credit requirements. Do not ship or service accounts beyond what you have set as your standard terms. (Of course, as noted earlier, you might have "net 30" printed on your invoice, but might not really expect people to pay you for 60 days because that is the standard in the industry.) Allow reorders to be shipped until an account reaches your standard limit--then freeze it, filling no more orders until the account is paid up.

Bearing all of the above in mind, however, you should still permit reasonable exceptions, such as a large account that is virtually completely paid up, but that still has a small percentage of invoices delayed for purely administrative reasons (such as paperwork is being tracked down or problems with an earlier order). In this case, it might be appropriate to extend more credit. Yet you should be wary when you get these paperwork ploys; it may be difficult to determine when these are legitimate excuses. Be open to the possibility of providing more credit, but beware of stalls.

Be especially cautious in giving credit to new businesses, since new businesses (as distinguished from new accounts) are, by nature, risky undertakings. A new business might have excellent credit references for year or two (while it is still primarily relying on its start-up capital). But then its credit rating may plummet when the "seed money" is exhausted, and the business must rely on lower-than-expected sales levels to pay bills.

You should be similarly cautious when dealing with certain industries that have many small firms prone to paying bills late. Such companies often appear to be undercapitalized and marginally profitable--but have been around for many years. In such a case, consider building sales by extending modest amounts of credit to such established firms, despite a history of paying bills somewhat late. Do not grant large amounts of credit to such a company. Remember, there is always a risk that marginal accounts will go out of business, no matter how well established they are.

Another high-risk area is very fast-growing customers who have fast-growing credit demands. These accounts, too, need to be watched carefully. On the one hand, such companies could build your sales and profits handsomely; on the other hand, they could deliver a devastating blow if their fast growth suddenly leads to serious financial trouble. A good way to reduce your risk is to get to know key personnel so that you can get an inside view of how things really are going at a given company. Watch statements, even if the company is currently paying bills on time. Adjust credit lines quickly if you sense a problem. Above all, do not ship products or services if these companies reach overdue status. Often you will find these fast-growing firms will pressure you to extend more and more credit as their payments become slower and slower. Resist the temptation! One large, fast-growing account that gets into trouble could cause a lot more damage than several smaller accounts that refuse to pay on the first order.

The more time you spend checking credit, the more precious cash you will conserve. You will avoid some customers who cannot real-istically be expected to pay you. You will avoid others who can be counted on to pay late--in essence, people who borrow money from you interest-free. And you will have minimized losses on active accounts. Careful credit checking is cash in your company's coffers!

CHAPTER 6:
Managing Consumer Credit Risks

Most small businesses do not extend credit to consumers beyond accepting major credit cards and checks. The reason is simple: extending credit is expensive and risky. Often, small businesses feel that they do not have to extend credit to consumers to be competitive.

Consider this: if you extend credit to all of your customers, and even one out of twenty fails to pay you, you will have lost five percent of your gross sales to bad debt. In many cases, such a bad debt ratio will trim your profits significantly--perhaps by as much as one half.

A five percent bad debt ratio is, unfortunately, not uncommon among businesses granting credit. And if you do not have a good credit and collection policy, your bad debt ratio could be even worse.

In granting credit, you will not only have to assume the cost of some bad debt, but also the cost and time of checking your firm's credit and collection activities. However, you must monitor these activities, unless you are willing to risk potentially catastrophic levels of bad debt.

Credit Cards

By far the easiest and cheapest solution for many small businesses is to make the acceptance of credit cards the only non-cash payment method. (Here, of course, we should note that many businesses consider personal checks as "cash", though checks, as we have seen, carry the risk of nonpayment if they bounce.)

When you do accept a credit card payment (and follow the appropriate procedures for verification), the credit card company becomes your credit department, and your bad debt worries are virtually eliminated. Although the fees the credit card company charges might seem high at first (they vary with your volume of business and average transaction size, but can range from about 2.5% to 5.5% of sales), these expenses are probably minimal when compared with the investment necessary to set up your own credit department. All policy decisions, credit checks, and collection work are assumed by the credit card company--as is, of course, whatever bad debt turns up despite careful checking. In addition, by having the credit card companies extend all of your credit, you will avoid having to tie up precious working capital in accounts receivable.

Setting Up a Credit Card Account

To accept credit cards, you need the appropriate merchant discount agreements with each of the companies whose cards you are going to take. In the case of MasterCard or Visa, you can work out arrangements through a commercial bank, though some banks have stricter policies than others for opening new accounts.

For instance, the larger banks commonly require that you actually have a store or retail business before they will even consider giving you an account; they don't want to deal with people operating businesses from their home. Your bank may make an exception if you have been with the bank for a long time--say five years or more. Otherwise, these larger banks believe your volume of business won't be large enough to justify having an account. They may also be afraid that if you are in a small home-based or mail-order business, you may have more problems than usual with bad cards, charge-backs or returned charges, and too little volume to warrant the effort involved.

For these reasons, you'll probably do better making arrangements through a smaller bank. Such banks may be receptive, even if you don't have an account there, because they are more eager to get your business. And they may open up an account for you provisionally, pending approval of your application.

At a bare minimum, you'll need a fictitious business name showing that you are a legitimate business, because the bank will want to open up a business account for you. You can apply at your county clerk's office for a doing-business-as (DBA) business name if you don't already have one.

You should also be aware that a business account will cost more than a personal one. The business account. for instance, will commonly require a higher minimum balance for no-check charges than a personal account. The typical cost might be five dollars a month plus check charges, unless there is a minimum balance of $1,000 or more in the account.

The Major Problems with Credit Cards

Assuming your application to use credit cards is approved, and you can take them, what pitfalls must you avoid?

Some places simply accept the customer's word that the card is good and requires only a signature. This, however, carries some risks.

For one thing, the card may be invalid. This can occur as a result of an old expiration date, because the card has been reported lost or stolen, or because it has been altered or counterfeited. Alternatively, the person may return the merchandise or dispute the charge, in which case you'll get a charge back on your account.

With new customers or clients, then, if you have any reason to question the card or the person's satisfaction with the transaction, do a little checking to protect yourself.

Check the name of the person on the card against other ID, and make sure signatures match.

Check the list of invalid cards which is regularly sent to merchant account holders. The list is updated regularly; if you accept a card on the list, you are responsible for the total charged.

A word on credit card fraud. If you discover that someone has a "hot card," you are supposed to take it away; you'll get a reward for doing this. But use your own judgment in confiscating cards. When you do a careful check against your invalid card list, someone who is actually trying to pass a bad card will generally leave quickly; the transaction then becomes a matter for the police. If the customer remains, and it looks like you'll face a battle if you try to retain the card, you may be better off returning it with a politely vague explanation. (For instance, "There's some problem verifying this; you'd better talk to your bank about it.") In this way, you avoid any misguided heroics, and can always call the police or card company later.

You might arrange for a credit card service you can call to check the status of a card. The service will not only use a computer to check the card's validity against a list of invalid cards, but will also have the latest updates a few days before you get them. If you do use such a service, be sure to verify, at the very least, all large or questionable purchases.

Write down additional information on the credit invoice you fill out; this will help you track down the person later if necessary. A driver's license number and a current address and phone number are both helpful.

Have the customer sign an agreement or release form for any merchandise received to indicate he or she is satisfied with the purchase and agrees to your procedures for collecting disputed funds. Should you find yourself in a charge-back dispute, you will then have more clout to back up your side when the credit card firm contacts you about the dispute.

Today, credit cards have become so much a part of doing business that many people think of these transactions as cash in the bank. Again, however, you don't have the money until the transaction clears. So protect yourself, or you may find that accepting credit cards costs you more than you can afford.

How to Offer In-House Credit Without Any Risk

If you feel strongly that you need to be able to offer consumers credit in addition to accepting credit cards, you might consider setting up an arrangement with an outside firm, such as a local bank or a finance company.

Using this approach, a consumer desiring credit would fill out an application in your office to buy goods from your firm--but the bank or finance company would actually assume the debt. You would simply deliver the credit application to the financial institution; if the the application is approved, the financial institution gives you cash when the consumer receives merchandise. As is the case with credit cards, you would pass the credit risk and collection work onto a third party--and improve your cash flow in the process.

Even some Fortune 500 companies prefer to have outside financial institutions provide consumer financing. Why? Even though these large companies have much easier access to financing than any small business, they would rather focus on delivering products and services than on financing consumers. You may have the same preference for your company.

Unfortunately, unless your small business is of a certain size (i.e., at or near one million dollars in sales yearly), and unless your product or service sells for at least several hundred dollars per unit, it will be difficult to find an outside financial institution willing to set up an in-house financing arrangement for you. If your business doesn't meet these criteria, you might consider developing an informal arrangement whereby you refer customers to a certain banker for financing.

Maximizing Your Cash-Based Transactions

If you decide that you must extend credit to be competitive in your industry, remember that you do not necessarily have to extend credit to all customers. Do as much business as you can on a cash basis; you might even want to offer a slight discount for payment by cash or check.

Consider your own experiences on this score. You've probably noticed, for instance, that many gas stations have two prices for their products: a low rate for cash purchases, and a higher rate for credit card purchases. As a general rule, you will improve cash flow and reduce your total costs by encouraging cash sales.

The Application

Before you extend credit, try to engage in some basic screening activities. Obtain and verify key facts about those to whom you are considering granting credit.

You will need to resolve certain questions. Where is the applicant employed? What salary does he or she earn? Does the applicant have enough discretionary income to make the payments on the purchase? How likely is it that the applicant will stay in the area or remain available until the debt is paid? What chance is there that the applicant may abandon the debt by leaving town before payments are completed?

To get the answers you need, have the applicant fill out a credit application that covers this information and other important facts. Note that a printed application keeps the process of extending credit formal and businesslike, and encourages the applicant to take the process seriously. Written forms are also helpful because the applicant might be embarrassed to reveal his or her income verbally, but will probably not hesitate to write down accurate information. Applicants are also less likely to exaggerate in writing. (A sample credit application appears below.)

The simple act of asking for the relevant information on a credit application will dramatically reduce your potential credit problems. Most people will pay debts they can afford to pay; in most cases, the application process will tell you whether or not the applicant can afford to make the proposed credit payments. Of course, this process will also help you minimize those cases where you extend credit to applicants who present unacceptable risks. In addition, this information will be useful in locating the person or his or her assets later, if the applicant subsequently does not pay.

In evaluating someone's income, try to determine the likelihood that the dollar levels will be sufficient to cover payments over the entire period you foresee financing. If the person's job background has been very stable, this is a good sign. But if there's anything about the person's work that suggests instability, proceed with caution. For example, if the applicant just obtained a new sales position in which payment is by commission only, income may fluctuate dramatically from one week to the next. Similarly, if the applicant just obtained a job paying a good salary, but did not work at all for the last six months, you will probably want to be cautious in extending credit: it is not inconceivable that the new position will be short-lived.

Knowing the applicant's income is not enough, however. Income figures can be misleading; what you really need to know is not just the applicant's total income, but his or her discretionary income as well. Discretionary income refers to the income remaining after unavoidable major fixed expenses (such as taxes, mortgage or rent, car payments, other loan payments, and alimony or child support payments). If the applicant does not have enough income to live comfortably after paying such fixed expenses, you should not extend credit. In such circumstances, an overextended applicant is likely to regard the debt to you as an "optional" item, or one that can be put off as circumstances demand.

But even if the applicant meets such income standards, other factors should be taken into account, such as time in the area. For example, you will probably not want to extend credit automatically to someone who has only recently moved to your community. Though exceptions are possible, the "recent arrival" does represent a significantly increased credit risk from a statistical standpoint, particularly if the person's past history is dotted with many short stints in a number of far-flung locales. Investigate such an applicant's background carefully before deciding to extend credit.

Of course, in evaluating information from the application, you cannot place complete trust in what every applicant tells you. Before you approve credit, verify the following with the applicant's employer:

1) The duration of the applicant's employment with the firm.

2) The income earned by the applicant.

3) The position the applicant holds.

If the applicant works in a large firm, you may need to call the firm's personnel office to confirm this information. If any data is not accurate, you should probably deny credit, even if the income criteria is still satisfactory. A person who puts false information on your credit application is likely to be a significant credit risk.

By going to the extra effort to verify this information, you will significantly reduce your chances of encountering a bad debt on the account. Not only will you be sure of the individual's income, as well as the length of time spent at his or her current job, but you will also know whether these portions of the credit application were filled out truthfully. And if they were, there's a good chance the rest of the information on the application is accurate as well.

Note that you will reduce the potential for friction with the prospective customer by calling your form something other than a "Credit Check"; you might consider "New Customer Data Profile," "Fact Sheet," or "Client Questionnaire."

NEW CLIENT QUESTIONNAIRE

Name:

Home Address:

City, State, Zip:

Business (if own business):

Employer (if employed):

Address:

City, State, Zip:

Phone:

Nearest relative/friend for emergencies:

Name:

Address:

City, State, Zip:

Phone:

Who referred you to us?

Do you: Own home   ?   Rent   ?

How long at last address?

Previous address if there less than 2 years:

If paying by check:

Bank Name:

Account #:

If paying by charge card:

Type of Card and Cardholder:

Account #:

If you are looking for a short cut, note that some small firms (and even some huge corporations), extend their own in-house credit to anyone who has a currently valid major credit card. The assumption is that if this person has passed someone else's credit check, there is no need to institute another. Such an assumption may not always be valid, however, because people with credit cards can easily become overburdened with debt, and therefore be less creditworthy. Nevertheless, the credit card check can serve as an easy, time-saving rule of thumb for many businesses.

Checking Credit and Bank References

Obviously, the more credit information you can obtain about an applicant, the better your credit decisions will be. However, checking individual references does consume time and money. For a relatively inexpensive purchase (under, say, $1,000) by an applicant with a solid employment background, you may want only to check employment history, and leave credit references unchecked. If, however, an applicant's employment history is weak, you might want to check credit references as well.

In any event, you should, as a general rule, ask for credit references, even if you know that you will not check them. Asking for these references serves an important function. If a person has no good credit references to list, he or she will probably either pay cash or skip the purchase altogether--a course of action you may regret in the short run, but that will keep you from building your sales on a shaky credit foundation.

Another good reference to request is the applicant's bank. If you decide to call the bank the applicant lists, however, don't expect to come away with too much relevant data. Unless the individual has a personal banker, you will probably only be able to obtain very rough average balance and account information. Banks will often provide little more than a cursory indication of the account's activity or size. For example, you may only be able to learn that the applicant has a "low four-figure average balance."

Credit Bureaus

When extending credit for a purchase of a significant amount (over $1000), it's a good idea to check with at least one, if not more, credit reporting services. In addition to helping you decide whether or not to provide credit, the information you receive from a credit service could help in later efforts to track down the individual (and his or her assets) if the account becomes delinquent.

The first section of the report lists the name of the person and when the first and last entries on the report were made. There follows a summary of the person's last three addresses, age, social security number, and recent places of employment. Next comes a rating of the number of credit accounts the person has had, and the balance of the highest and lowest accounts. This summary indicates the status of the different accounts based on a rating system such as the following:

0: too new to rate
1: paid as agreed
2-6: one to six months late
7: Chapter 13 bankruptcy
8: reposession
9: written off

The report also includes a listing of secured loans and judgments; inquiries about the account; and a detailed listing of stores, banks, and others who have provided credit.

The Balance Sheet

If you are extending credit for a larger ticket item, you should consider asking the customer to provide you with a balance sheet. This lists a person's assets (such as bank accounts, property, and automobiles) and liabilities (such as mortgages, loans, and credit card balances). An accurately filled out balance sheet will quickly tell you the net worth of an individual. (See the sample balance sheet that follows.)

SIMPLE BALANCE SHEET FOR AN INDIVIDUAL CONSUMER

Assets

Checking Account   _____

Savings Account   _____

Certificate
of Deposit   _____

Bonds   _____

Common Stocks   _____

Real Estate
(net of depreciation)   _____

Automobile   _____

Other Assets   _____

TOTAL   _____

Liabilities

Taxes   _____

Credit Card
Balances   _____

Mortgage   _____

Automobile Loan   _____

Other Loans   _____

Other Liabilities   _____

Net Worth   _____

TOTAL   _____

In assessing the creditworthiness of an individual, you should generally put more emphasis on income than net worth. A person with a great deal of equity built up in real estate may have a high net worth, but little discretionary income or cash; such a person might have difficulty meeting payments. Even if the person was forced to sell real estate to make payments to you, you would probably be in for a very long wait, and if the person doesn't pay you voluntarily, you will have to engage in costly collection procedures.

Setting Up Your Own Rating System

One way to streamline your credit decisions is to establish a rating system that takes most subjective judgments out of the process. With such a system, even the most inexperienced clerk can make relatively sound credit decisions instantly. You will find this approach especially appropriate when you are granting relatively small amounts of credit, and when a number of different people must make credit decisions. (Of course, you can use any credit rating system as an additional piece of credit information--to help you make an even more careful, considered judgment.)

In setting up your own credit rating system, you must be careful not to discriminate against minority groups, women, handicapped persons, or other groups. One reason not to institute discriminatory practices is that these practices are not good for business, since they can give you a bad reputation and reduce your potential market. In addition, even the appearance of bias on your part could result in a costly lawsuit. So don't use race, sex, or age in setting up your rating system or in making credit decisions. (Other business decisions can also sometimes be considered discriminatory. For example, some banks have been charged with discrimination for "redlining"--refusing to extend credit, typically home mortgage loans--in certain city neighborhoods.

The following is a hypothetical credit rating system; adapt it to your own business environment. For example, if you are selling expensive mink coats, you might want to categorically deny credit to anyone who does not already have a major credit card, a checking or savings account, and a phone at home.

SAMPLE SCORING SYSTEM

	Points
Years at present residence:	
Up to 2 years	1
2-5 years	2
More than 5 years	3
Years at present job:	
Less than 1 year	1
1-3 years	2
4-6 years	3
7 or more years	5
Spouse or significant other employed	2
Monthly obligations (including rent or mortgage):	
Less than $1,000	2
Over $1,000	1
Type of work:	
Professionals, executive	4
Skilled worker	3
Blue collar	2
All others	1
Loan experience:	
at a bank where you apply for a loan	5
at another bank	3
Checking or savings account at bank where you want credit	2

To use the sample credit rating system, simply add up the points. If the applicant scores over twelve, you are probably justified in extending a modest amount of credit. (Note: do not "tally things up" and reach your decision in front of the customer; you are likely to create a lot of unnecessary tension if credit is denied.)

Managing Risks

Extending credit to consumers entails risk and expense. If you can avoid extending credit altogether, do so; accepting major credit cards is often a workable alternative. If you do decide to extend credit on your own, be sure to conduct an appropriate credit check. This will ultimately save time and money, and help you avoid needless aggravation.

CHAPTER 7:
Pre-Collection
Questions

In order to collect any debt effectively, large or small, there are several key principles to keep in mind.

Follow up quickly--as soon as you see that the debt is overdue.

Follow up consistently, so that the debtor gets used to hearing from you regularly. This reaffirms the obligation and gives the debtor a fair opportunity to air any dispute.

Start with the assumption that the debtor is an honorable, responsible person who only needs to be reminded about the debt. Treat him or her in a friendly, respectful way. Then gradually build up the pressure by acting more firmly and expressing more and more urgency that the debt be paid.

Be careful to follow the legal and ethical guidelines for debt collecting. You don't want to end up owing more to the debtor than he or she does to you because of your inappropriate collection practices.

Seek payment in full (or payments when due) if you can, but be flexible enough to accept alternate arrangements.

Even if you have a written agreement, reestablish the validity of the debt, in case you have to go to court. Do this by phone, in the letters you write, when you meet, and, ideally, with a second promissory note reaffirming the debt.

If you don't already have a written agreement, get the debtor to sign a promissory note for the debt. That reaffirms the debt so that there can be no dispute about it. Then, if you have to go to court, the process will be very simple, and the note can provide for interest and attorney's costs.

See yourself as someone who seeks to work with the debtor to help him or her to pay the debt, once he or she agrees it is rightfully due. Avoid taking the role of the debtor's adversary. Work on motivating the debtor to pay through appeals to basic human needs--like pride, self-respect, and self-interest.

Work out your own system for following up to collect debts in a timely fashion--then follow that system. Whether you are one individual collecting from another or a company collecting from a large business, the principle is the same--you need a consistent, effective system to get the money you are owed.

Unless things appear hopeless, try to maintain good will while you work on getting your money. This way you can continue to work together when the collection process is over.

Using these principles will work whether you're an individual or a business. While a business may need a more formal debt collection system using these principles--and some even use the computer--the collection process still works the same way.

Don, a professional collector for an insurance company, used many of these techniques in collecting overdue accounts for his company. "The important thing is consistency," Don emphasized. "When someone owes us money, I remind them a few days after it's overdue, and then I call them every three or four days until they come to expect it. In fact, some of them don't even answer the phone. When I reach them, I say I want to work with them, and offer to see what we can arrange. Normally, I invite them to come down to the office to see what we can work out. I say I'd like to get them to agree to as much as possible so they can get it over with. But I want to make sure they can afford it, and I tell them this, because otherwise I'll be calling them again, if they don't keep their promise.

"Then I make sure to get everything in writing and have them sign another agreement indicating what they will pay when. I find it's best to get them involved in the process so they feel they are working things out themselves. It's not just me telling them this is the way it's going to be. Finally, I keep track of the excuses, and if it's the same one several times, I call them on it. So they see they can't put one over on me, because I'm on top of the situation.

"Eventually, they realize they have to pay--it's what they agreed-- and they do."

Setting Up Your Collection System

When you set up a collection system, the time line for various types of collection activities can vary depending on the size of the debt, whether it's a personal or a business debt, and other factors. But basically, once a debt becomes overdue, the collection process goes through these phases, which can end any time--when the debt is paid or when you give up on the debt.

The Four Stages

There are four basic phases, outlined below.

The notification or polite reminder stage (sometimes referred to as the "nudge").

The formal appeals and discussion stage.

The push or firm demand stage.

The "squeeze" or "bitter end" stage. Here there are several alternatives: a collection agency; an attorney (if the account is large enough); or small claims or municipal court. This final stage may involve a single alternative or perhaps a combination of them, depending on the difficulty of collection and the size of the debt.

A good way to set up a system is to use these four stages as a guideline and establish a time line indicating when you will move from stage to stage. You can use the same time line for all of your debts or vary it for different types of debts (i.e., debts from individual customers, debts from suppliers, and debts from personal friends and associates) or for debts of different sizes (say, under $100, from $100-1,500, from $1,500-5,000, and over $5,000).

You might write off accounts under $50; refer those from $50-200 to a collection agency; take those from $200-1,500 to small claims court; file those from $1,500-5,000 in municipal court yourself (you won't need an attorney if the case is clear cut, with a firm contract or promissory note); and take to an attorney those over $5,000.

Plan to start your time line running within a few days to a maximum of 30 days after the payment is due. The sooner you start the better, usually, though some individuals and companies prefer a longer grace period. Getting started early is a more powerful reminder that you are serious--and the debtor has less time to file and forget.

The Time Line

The date that an account is due, sometimes called the "maturity date," can be established in a number of ways--verbally or by a promissory note, contract, or bill or sale. (For example, the promissory note or contract may specify that payment is due by March 15, 1991; or a bill of sale may state that payment is due within five, ten, fifteen, or thirty days after delivery. If you can, go for a shorter payment date after delivery.)

However you establish this date, once the account is due, you have a right to payment, and any payment not received is overdue. At this point, many creditors wait 30 days to send out their first notification that the account is due. If you wait, you simply give the debtor a longer period in which to pay. Thus, it's better to get started right away. Five days to a week is normally enough. If the debtor has put a check in the mail, you should have gotten it by then, and if not, he or she is late.

What Next?

Once you are ready to take action on an overdue account, the *Notification/Reminder Stage* begins. Your assumption at this stage should be that the debtor has made a mistake and has forgotten about the bill. Typically, you can plan on sending out a brief notification letter, reminder note, or perhaps make a short phone call to remind the debtor. Then plan to wait about fifteen days before sending out another letter or two or making one or two more calls. For most creditors, letters are more common at this stage, but some use phone calls. Ideally, space each of these contacts about two weeks apart. This whole stage should last about 30 days.

Some companies or individuals are more aggressive in taking legal action at this point, and if they have no response to their letters or calls may send one final notice before suit. One approach with the bigger debts might be to use a quick process that moves directly from the notification/reminder stage to the final demand in about 45-60 days in this way: a letter reminder; then a mailgram requesting payment; then a phone call or personal visit; and a final demand. This approach can work well with accounts involving large debts where the sum is clearly due, where there's a contract or promissory note, and where the account is worth taking to court.

If you have a small debt, however, this approach may not be appropriate. In these cases it's usually more cost effective to motivate the debtor to pay, retain good will, and stay out of court.

Creditors typically avoid appearing overly aggressive during this initial stage, and are relatively patient. The ideas is to work out a payment arrangement and still preserve the business, friendship, or customer relationship. The delays may feel frustrating, but most creditors accept them at this point.

If the notification/reminder stage proves ineffective, the *Appeals/Discussion Stage* begins. At this point, the creditor has to do more than just remind the debtor; now the creditor has to motivate the debtor to pay and try to discover if there is any problem behind the debtor's failure to do so. Your assumption now should be that the debtor knows about the debt but can't or won't pay.

Accordingly, you should focus in this phase on assisting and working things out with the debtor. Since brief reminders haven't worked, you now need to make one or more appeals using individually written letters, telephone calls, or, in some cases, personal visits. Although seeing the debtor in person is usually the most effective way to deal with the problem, it may not be economically feasible. So creditors generally rely on phone calls and letters. If there is an ongoing business relationship, this is usually the time when creditors cut off additional credit. Depending on the situation, this stage can last between 15 to 45 days.

Once it appears that appeals and discussion haven't worked, it's time for the *Push or Firm Demand Stage* (commonly about 45-90 days after starting the collection process). Your assumption is still that the debtor can't or won't pay, so now you are making a single, last-ditch effort to tell the debtor that you are about to give up, that it is urgent the debtor pay up at once or you will take the next step of turning the matter over to a lawyer, a professional collector, or the courts. Generally, creditors making this demand send a certified letter restating the debt, review their efforts to collect, and state what they intend to do if the debtor doesn't respond by a certain date (usually within 10 days).

If the debtor still doesn't pay, it's time to move to the *Bitter End Stage*, where you take the threatened action. Each action has some advantages and disadvantages, depending upon the size and nature of the debt, and we'll discuss them in depth in a later chapter on your options for getting tough to collect difficult debts. Briefly, a lawyer will typically send out one or two demand letters or make a call or two before filing suit. A collection agency will try to motivate the debtor through appeals and discussion--which is much like the regular appeals process, though more intense, since a professional third-party collector is involved; if that doesn't work, the agency may file suit or turn the case back to you. If you go to court yourself, you can speed up the process of initiating litigation.

If you do win at court, you still have to collect, a process that can take a great deal of time and effort if the debtor still doesn't pay.

The time frames we've outlined are commonly used by individuals and companies trying to collect from customers, clients, and other businesses. You can shorten or lengthen the process as is best for you.

For instance, if you're trying to collect from an individual retail store patron and see the person every week, you might wait only a week between reminders and appeals instead of the usual 15 days. Each time you see the debtor you can demonstrate your insistence on collecting what's due and thereby shorten the time to collect. If you don't say anything about the debt on the alternate weeks when you see each other, you may lose your clout. On the other hand, if you have learned that a businessperson who owes you money is going through hard times, it may make sense to wait. You might touch bases with the person occasionally, to let him know you still expect to be paid, but you don't want to come on too strong like a heartless Simon Legree.

In short, set up general guidelines for moving from one phase in the collection process to another. Then adapt your timeline to the circumstances and nature of the debt.

CHAPTER 8:
Keeping Track of
Overdue Accounts

Once you have established when accounts become overdue and set up a time line for follow-up, you need a system to advise you about these times so that you can swing into action with letters, phone calls, or personal contact. You will still treat each debtor individually, since you have to find ways to motivate the debtor and work out any payment problems on a case-by-case basis. But your system will let you know when it's time to act, as you gradually increase the pressure from simple reminders to firmer efforts to collect.

Essentially, this system keeps a record of all past-due bills on a daily basis so you know exactly how long each account is overdue. Then, when you review the records for that account, you can establish easily what you have done so far to collect. Some companies are so systematic about this process that they have developed a series of collection letters designed to be sent out at specific times. The creditor can personalize the process as necessary by adding personal notes to these letters, and can also use a phone call, mailgram, or personal meeting instead of sending a letter.

There are several effective follow-up methods to consider.

The Ledger System. This is based on your daily books, which list the sales made and indicate which ones have payments due. You use succeeding columns in the ledger to indicate when you take steps to collect past due funds. It's an excellent, simple system if you are a small businessperson, retailer, or professional and only have a small number of accounts, since you can keep all of the records in one place. Then you review the records from time to time to find out which accounts are overdue and take the appropriate action.

However, the system can become a problem if you have a large number of accounts, because it is difficult to check the records constantly. Moreover, the system can fall apart if you get very busy and check the records only occasionally. If you decide to use this system, you have to check through the books regularly--at least once a week--to keep current with your accounts.

The Card Tickler System. This works well when you have a large number of accounts, whether clients, suppliers, or customers. The system involves using a special file in which you make a card for each overdue account, listing information about the bill--amount, terms, when due, and what you've done to collect so far. You divide up the file into a number of compartments--31 if you plan to review the cards for delinquencies each day, fewer if you expect to do your review every two or three days. Date each compartment to indicate when to take action on the cards in that section. When you do your review, check each card against the ledger. If it's still unpaid, take some action, note this on the card, and move the card ahead in the file to your next review period-- perhaps 15 days later. If the bill is paid, as noted in the ledger, remove the card and either destroy it or put it in an archive file--just in case the debtor gets into trouble again.

The advantage of this system is that it brings the delinquent files to your attention so you can handle them in a standardized way. There is one disadvantage: you end up with two sets of records on overdue accounts, and have to check back and forth between the cards and the ledger.

One way around this might be to use cards in place of a ledger to record all payments. File the cards for paid-up accounts in chronological order, just as you might record payments in a ledger, placing unpaid account cards into the tickler system. Should a customer, client, or supplier run up additional bills, use another card to record these and clip together all cards for a single individual or company in both files.

The Duplicate Invoice System. This system is most appropriate when you send out bills to your customers or clients in addition to recording payments, and when you have a large number of accounts that become overdue. Whenever you send out a bill, keep an extra copy in the duplicate files, which you can arrange like the tickler system. When the bill is paid, pull the duplicate invoice from the file and destroy it.

The system makes sense when many of your bills are overdue. If you don't deal with many late payments, of course, you are doing twice the filing work for no particular reason. (At the same time, if you have so many overdue accounts that you need a double record system, it may be time to ask yourself why so many people don't pay right away, and perhaps tighten things up.)

Using a Manual or Computer System

You can use these systems manually or you can put your collections program on a computer. The right system can record your sales or receipts, type out bills, keep track of overdue accounts, print out collection letters, let you know when to make a collection call, and keep notes of the account's history. Whether you use it as a ledger, card-tickler/ledger system, or duplicate invoice system, your computer can streamline everything you do. Using a computer can be particularly efficient when you have numerous accounts. If you own a personal computer, you should consider checking with your local software dealer for recommendations on an accounts receivable system.

CHAPTER 9:
The Dos and Don'ts
of Debt Collecting

Before you actively launch into a debt-collecting campaign, you must be aware of what you can and cannot do. Ill-informed efforts to collect may result in more legal costs for you than the debt itself.

When you are trying to collect your own debts, you work under fewer restrictions, since many guidelines on debt collection apply to the actions of third parties (like business credit departments or collection agencies, which are heavily regulated by both Federal and State laws). But even so, there are many laws designed to protect the debtor from undue harassment and public embarrassment.

In the beginning stages of the collection process, you aren't likely to run afoul of these laws. Nevertheless, you should know what they are, for one stage can rapidly move into another, particularly if you begin to initiate personal contact. For example, you might start off the meeting by issuing a simple reminder, and watch things quickly escalate to an appeal, a discussion, a dispute, and perhaps a threat to go to court.

Certainly, collecting some debts can be so frustrating that creditors may be tempted to use some of the old (and illegal) standbys of the past: calling the debtor at all hours of the night; telling the debtor's friends he or she is a deadbeat, making threatening calls to the debtor's boss; even warning the debtor to pay up . . . or else.

Remember, though, that all those tactics are illegal and can get you sued or arrested. And in the long run, the approach of motivating and assisting the debtor to pay works better. For the most part, debtors want to pay if they can, once they acknowledge and accept the debt. Your role is to motivate them in a legal, dignified way.

A dramatic (if unusual) example of what can happen when a creditor tries to go outside the law is this story of a bail bondsman who turned a minor collection dispute into a $100,000 debt--and lost his business as a result.

The bail bondsman had bailed out a prostitute for $500 on a $50 bond. When she didn't show up for the hearing, the bondsman looked to be out $500--but instead of accepting that as the breaks of the game, the bondsman decided to track down the prostitute himself for another court hearing so he wouldn't have to pay. He hired three tough cohorts to bring her in; they attempted to do so with a flourish. When they arrived at the woman's apartment, they pulled out their guns and announced that the woman answering the door was under arrest. Unfortunately, it turned out that the bondsman had arranged for the "arrest " of the wrong woman. When she sued, the bondsman ended up owing $100,000. He didn't pay right away, and her lawyer appointed a receiver for his business.

Other creditors have been hauled into court when they have resorted to libel, harassment, theft, or other illegal techniques to collect their debt. One manufacturer, for example, lost his business and ended up owing $200,000 because he tried to blackball his debtor with other manufacturers, staged a picket in front of the man's shop, and tried to help himself to some merchandise to pay the debt.

The Wild West is over as far as collections go; nowadays the process is heavily regulated. The primary law is the Fair Debt Collection Practices Act (Public Law 95-109) passed in 1977. This act applies not only to anyone who regularly collects debts for a living but to anyone who, in collecting his own debts, uses any name other than his own to suggest a third party is involved. This means collection departments in businesses are covered too; furthermore, if you bring in a friend to help you with a personal debt, the law applies. If you go it alone, you have more leeway, but you are still subject to laws covering harassment and abuse, falsehoods and misrepresentation, profane, obscene, or abusive language, and libel, slander, and character assassination.

So what, exactly, can't you do to collect a debt?

No Falsehoods, Misrepresentation, or Deceptive Practices

This is mandated by two federal laws: the Federal Trade Commission Act and the Fair Debt Collection Act. (In addition, many state laws are quite tough, permitting both damages and attorney's fees for unfair or deceptive collection activities.) Under these provisions, there are a number of things you can't do.

You can't pretend you are someone other than who you are or use other deceptive means to collect a debt unless you are involved in skip tracing (tracking down a debtor). However, you can use an alias.

You can't use a fake identity on a letterhead or in a phone call, although as an individual you have more leeway than the third-party collector. After all, your "new identity" could be a side business you have created.

You can't imply that you are an attorney or a federal or state government agent or that you work for a credit reporting bureau or collection agency when you do not.

You can't send out collection notices that look like official court summonses or documents. You can buy these notices in some stationery supply stores, but don't. If your debtor actually believes the document is real, he or she will probably turn it over to an attorney, and you're likely to face a countersuit in court.

You can't suggest the debtor has committed a crime by not paying the debt.

You can't threaten to turn the account over to your "legal department for collection" if you don't have a legal department.

You can't threaten to do anything other than turn the case over to a collection agency or attorney, or to file suit. Furthermore, you can't make this threat unless you're actually going to do it. If you threaten to take a specific collection action and don't do it, that's misrepresentation. And if you threaten certain actions, like notifying other creditors, telling the debtor's employer or friends, threatening to file criminal charges against the debtor, or publishing his name on a list of deadbeats, you might be involved in extortion. You definitely don't want that.

You can't charge excessive interest on the debt; that's committing usury.

You can't inflate the debt so the debtor thinks he or she owes more than the actual debt. You can always try to get a bit extra when you take the debtor to court and want to sue for damages, interest, or emotional distress. But if you make your bill excessive and provoke a response, you might find your debtor suing you.

You also can't plead that you didn't intend to deceive if you are caught by your debtor in one of these practices and he or she decides to sue. All you have to do is deceive the debtor, and that's enough.

No Harassment or Abuse

In the old days, creditors could do just about everything (and did) to make life miserable for the debtor, including threatening to hurt the debtor and his property or reputation. Now any sort of harassment and abuse are out. However, since there is a fine line between contacting and harassing or abusing someone, the courts often require that the debtor warn you to stop doing something before they will consider it harassment.

The kinds of activities to avoid here are easy enough to recognize. They are outlined in detail below; while you will probably come across stories of creditors who use such techniques and obtain payment, be aware that the debtor will probably have grounds for criminal action if you cross the line.

You can't make repeated phone calls. You can only call once a day if you reach the person you want. You can call a business back until you reach the person who writes the check, unless someone tells you that person is away or will be busy for some time. Then you have to wait a reasonable time to call again.

You can't let the phone ring and ring.

You can't make calls very early in the morning or very late at night to the debtor's home, unless you know he or she is a shift worker. (The usual policy followed by collectors is not to call before 8 a.m. or after 9 p.m.) But you can call a business any time during business hours.

You can't make calls to a person at work, if he or she doesn't want you to call there, and you can't call a business owner at home, if he or she asks you to call at the business only.

You can't pretend you're someone else so you can call again and again.

You can't make obscene phone calls.

You can't threaten violence or harm to the debtor's property, person, or reputation.

You can't threaten members of the debtor's family.

You can't make physical threats. Of course, physical attack of any kind is out of the question: otherwise you're liable for assault.

You can't visit the consumer or businessperson and refuse to leave when asked. Of course, you can go and visit; but if the debtor tells you to go away, do so. Otherwise, you're trespassing and harassing the debtor, and he or she can press charges.

No Ruining the Debtor's Reputation

As much as you may feel like telling the world the debtor is a deadbeat, you can't, although on a selective, one-on-one basis, you probably will have no problem warning friends and business associates. After all, people do casually talk about others during conversation, and occasionally, people might ask what you think of someone. Or perhaps the press might do a piece on a notorious debtor who vanished without a trace. (For example, when a small-town travel promoter skipped town owing money to dozens of people, the local press did a story using interviews with some of the people who got bad checks and filed suit in small claims court.) However, you have to be careful about being too public with your statements or written comments. Libel and slander laws can be devastating. All the debtor has to show is that you made a defamatory statement to a third person who either heard or read your remark, and he or she may have grounds for an action against you.

Some of the libelous or slanderous activities you must avoid are summarized below.

You can't publish the names of debtors to show they owe you money.

You can't send the debtor a postcard mentioning an overdue debt (although you can send one for a regular payment notice), and you can't indicate anything on the envelope suggesting that the correspondence is a dunning notice. You can't do this because then you are, in effect, publishing or making a public statement about the debt. In fact, even a sealed letter addressed to the debtor can open you up for a libel action, if it is likely that your communication might be opened by a third person such as a secretary. If you write at all to someone at a business, mark it PERSONAL or PERSONAL AND CONFIDENTIAL to be safe. (If your confidential letter is accidentally read by a third person, that's okay. There's no law broken by an accidental communication to a third person.) Likewise, you can't send around telegrams, pictures, photographs, cartoons, tapes, or other materials you have prepared to embarrass the debtor.

You can't talk about the debt to anybody at the debtor's place of employment.

You can't discuss the debt with others, although you can contact people once to find out if they know where the debtor lives or works.

You can't call the debtor names, like "deadbeat" or "crook." Unless the debtor has actually been charged as such and convicted, you're committing libel. Likewise, you can't imply the debtor is such things by using circumlocutions or suggestive statements, such as, "I don't think he's honest." And you can't make unfounded conclusions you can't prove, such as: "He doesn't have very good credit."

Now, if in the course of ordinary conversation (as opposed to your efforts to collect money), you do make true statements to others about the debtor, there's no libel, because your statements are true, and you're not engaging in a public vendetta to embarrass the debtor. My own feeling is you should feel free to share your observations with other people selectively and quietly and give them information that might protect them from making a similar misjudgment. Although an attorney might make a case for saying nothing (since if the debtor sues, the burden will be on you to prove the truthfulness of your statement, which may be costly in time, effort, and money) in most instances it's unlikely that the debtor is going to protest. After all, if your observations are true, the debtor is probably going to want to be as quiet as possible about the situation so he or she can continue to get credit from others.

No Invasion of Privacy

You also have to avoid intruding unreasonably into the debtor's private affairs when you try to collect the debt.

You can't use the debtor's name or furnish information about him or her without permission. There are certain exceptions, since you do have the right to give credit or financial information to individuals and groups with a specific interest in obtaining this information, such as credit reporting agencies, credit interchange clubs, other creditors, prospective suppliers, and the customer's bank or other lending institutions. Unless a customer has specifically asked you not to disclose this information, you can provide it, and with credit reporting bureaus, you may provide it without such permission.

You can't look through records, reports, and letters that belong to the debtor in order to gain information on his financial situation unless you have permission to do so.

Many creditors surreptitiously seek to locate records about the debtor to get the information they need to effect service or find assets. Be aware of the risks if you get caught, however, because the debtor can always sue.

Conversely, you may want to give other creditors or credit services information in return for the information they give. In this case, you can legally do so as long as the person is an interested party with a right to know, and you state only the facts without drawing your own conclusions. (For example, you can talk about the credit line you have offered, the unpaid balance, the usual rate at which the customer pays, and the like without any problem. Then, let the person to whom you give this information decide whether to give credit or not.)

CHAPTER 10:
Effective Letters, Phone Calls, and Meetings with the Debtor

Once you know you have a collection problem, you've got to start motivating the debtor to pay through letters, phone calls and personal meetings. Though you will need to become firmer and firmer as the collection process continues, the basics of effective communication remain the same. We'll focus on those basics in this chapter. Subsequent chapters will deal with how to employ these principles in each phase of the process.

The Basic Technique for Motivating Action

To get someone to do anything, you must make sure the person understands the situation, recognizes why it is good to take action, and has a clear idea of what to do. It's the same in collecting money. The debtor has to be motivated to pay you or you won't get paid.

You might consider the whole collection process as a form of sales. You are trying to persuade the debtor to do something you want; in effect, you are trying to sell the debtor on paying you.

Just as a sales person tries to convince a prospect to buy, you have to look for the debtor's "hot buttons," the arguments that will get him or her to pay. For some people, appeals to survival and safety will work. ("Pay now and we'll continue to give you credit." "Pay now, or you'll lose your good credit rating." "If you don't pay, we'll take you to court.") For other people, appeals based on a desire for love and belonging are most effective. ("I thought I was your friend, but if you don't pay me..." "You've been a valued customer for many years. We'd hate to lose you now because of this problem with a small bill." "I hope we can work things out amicably so we can go on being friends.")

Still others respond most strongly to the need for pride and self-esteem. ("Like most people, you probably want to keep your good reputation as a responsible businessperson." "You've been trying to set a good example for others in your community. We hope you will want to continue to show your responsibility in this matter, too.")

And others will find appeals to self-fulfillment or self-actualization most convincing. ("We know ideals like integrity and loyalty are extremely important to you. Thus, we're sure you'll agree that this small matter should be taken care of. We trusted you when we gave you a loan; now we are trusting you to pay.")

Using this approach, it's best to start off with positive appeals first and urge the debtor to pay on the basis of cooperation, fair play, justice, and personal pride. If those don't work, you can go to your arsenal of negative appeals based on the debtor's self-interest and fear of reprisals (all legal, of course). For example, you can stress the difficulties the debtor and his or her loved ones may encounter when he or she doesn't pay. ("You know, if this case goes to court and you default, we will be able to call in the marshal or sheriff to levy against your property and bank account or garnish your wages.")

Writing Effective Letters

If you have more than a few bad debts, the collection letter is central to the collection process. Although one-on-one meetings and telephone calls have more impact, they take more time than letters, and if the debtor lives or works some distance away, the letter is more practical. In fact, some collection companies use a letter-writing approach exclusively with good results. For example, the Credit Network reports a 56 percent success rate in sending out a series of three to five collection letters of increasing intensity when the creditor's initial efforts have not worked.

Ideally, you should write your own letters and let your personal style show through, although if you are convinced you can't write your own letter, you can find all sorts of prewritten credit and collection letters in some specialized publications. Check your local bookstore.

But before you get overwhelmed trying to find just the right letter written by someone else, I think it's better to understand the basic principles for writing effective collection letters and put your ideas in your own words. Accordingly, in the following discussion of the collection process, the sample letters are primarily designed as examples. Adapt the ideas to your own personal style if you can.

Major Pointers for Good Letters

Keep your letter short; only one sheet of paper. When it's short, people are more likely to read it and act immediately. If you send a long letter, people are more apt to glance at it and put it on a pile of things to get to later.

Make your writing brief, to the point, and snappy, as if it were written by an advertising copywriter. Your letter should pack punch and motivate someone to do something, just as ads do.

Give your letter eye appeal so it's easy to read. Keep your paragraphs and sentences short for easy reading. Preferably, limit sentences to 22 words or less, and paragraphs to two sentences with a maximum of 6 lines or less. If your sentences are too long, people forget what you said in the beginning of the sentence. If your paragraphs and sentences look too unwieldly, no one will read them.

Even if you are writing to a friend, type your letter. It looks more impressive, and a typed letter will hold more weight if you have to go to court. Use large margins (1" to 1 1/2" on either side) so that you have plenty of white space. If a letter looks attractive and easy to read, it will make a more powerful statement. Center your letter on the page, so it doesn't crowd at the top or bottom.

Choose your words carefully for maximum impact. Avoid large words where possible: little words have more impact. Avoid complex or passive constructions, because simplicity and action words are more powerful. You know what it's like to get a letter in bureaucratese. People throw in dozens of long-winded phrases because they think it sounds more impressive. Forget it!   This kind of writing only serves to confuse and obscure. You want people to get your message right away and ACT!

Try to avoid beginning the first sentence in a paragraph with any references to yourself such as "I," "we," "my," and "our." Your first word sets the tone for the paragraph, and you want to avoid sounding self-centered. Emphasize your concern for the other person's point of view. Start paragraphs with words like "you," "your company," or use neutral words and phrases like, "Everyone needs good credit today."

Set the tone of your letter to encourage the debtor's positive response. Add a P.S. or special note to reemphasize a major point in your letter or personalize it. P.S.'s are good for underlining your proposal or desired action, because when people skim a letter, they tend to read the first paragraph, then the P.S. Also, you can use the P.S. for a personal note, to show you're still receptive to being friendly despite your firm, cool tone. "Hope you had a good vacation skiing; now that you're back, let's get this resolved."

As an alternative to putting a P.S. on the bottom of the letter, you can write it on a removable adhesive note and stick it on the letter. In this case, it's a good idea to use handwriting for both contrast and a personal touch. This encourages people to read your note . . . and then the letter.

Keep your letter courteous and tactful (though you should use increasing firmness as the debt continues to remain unpaid). You want to treat the debtor with respect, and if possible, retain his or her good will. You're more likely to get paid this way, than if you come on tough and make the debtor angry.

Use diplomatic expressions, at least in the early stages, to describe the overdue account. For example, talk about the account being "past due," a neutral statement of fact, rather than saying the debtor or account is "delinquent," which has a criminal ring.

Treat the debtor with respect, so he or she can maintain his or her pride. Thus, avoid accusing the debtor directly, and offer a way out, so he or she can explain the problem and maintain face. For example, you might say something like, "We understand how problems can develop that can interfere with your ability to pay a bill. But we do expect a full payment within 30 days and will be looking forward to getting our payment from you, since it is now overdue."

Avoid something like, "You agreed to pay our bill within 30 days in the contract you signed. But now it's delinquent, so we'll expect your payment within 10 days."

Organizing Your Letter

Keep in mind that your letter has three major parts: the opening, body, and close. Each section can be used effectively for certain purposes.

The Opening

Start the opening so that it immediately: gets the attention of the debtor; briefly presents the situation and indicates it is serious, without making the debtor angry; seeks to preserve the debtor's good will; and makes the debtor want to read on to find out what he or she can do about the situation.

A question can pull the debtor quickly into your letter. Alternatively, you may wish to use a strong statement as a lead in.

"Didn't you get our invoice of May 5th for $150?" "Are you having trouble paying our $300 bill? We'd like to help you get this matter resolved." "Your expected payment of $300 for the furniture you bought from us never arrived. We'd like to clear matters up, before we have a serious problem." "You've always been responsible in paying your bills with us. Now we have a small bill for $100 on your account that needs to be cleared up."

Avoid long-winded, commonly used expressions that lower reader interest, such as: "In looking over our records, we have discovered that..." "We have recently had it called to our attention that..." "We appreciate your previous letter about your account, but..."

The Body of Your Letter

In the body of your letter, explain the problem further, if necessary, and tell the debtor what you propose he or she do. Back up your proposal with the reason to do it.

"Your payment needs to be in our office by Monday, June 15, to clear our books and keep us from taking further action. We know you want to keep your good credit rating, and we'd like to help you do it."

"Let's set up a meeting to discuss how you can pay this account, if you are having trouble meeting your bills as you say. I know you want to deal with this problem responsibly, and I'd like to work with you so we can handle this together. You have been a valued customer, and this way we can get this matter resolved amicably."

"You've been a good friend for many years. Let's not let a little financial problem get in the way. I always thought you were someone to take care of your financial obligations quickly, and when I made the loan to you, you thought it was a great favor, and I trusted you."

A typical collection letter will contain the following arguments, adapted to your particular situation:

(1) The account is now overdue, or the account has been overdue for some time, and the creditor has previously contacted the debtor one or more times about this situation.

(2) The debtor should send or bring in a payment immediately.

(3) Unless the debtor acts, the creditor will have to take further action, such as stopping other credit, withdrawing friendship and goodwill, or taking legal action. (But don't threaten any action that you do not plan to carry through.)

(4) The creditor does not want to take these actions and would like to maintain the debtor's good will if possible.

(5) It is to the debtor's advantage to act now, because he or she will . . . (continue to enjoy a good reputation, keep a good credit rating, maintain the creditor's good will, etc.)

(6) If the debtor has any explanation or questions to raise about the amount, he or she should do so now.

In the early stages of the collection process, you can use a more casual, friendly, informal, or even chatty tone, as appropriate, to notify and remind the debtor about the debt and appeal to his or her self-interest. Gradually, if the debtor doesn't pay, your tone will shift to make the letter sound more intense and urgent.

The Closing

The purpose of the closing is to get the debtor to take action. You may have already told the debtor what you would like him or her to do, but emphasize it again: *the debtor should act now and make the payment that is due!*

Specifically, close by stating: what the debtor should do (pay X dollars); when the debtor should do it (today, so the payment arrives by a certain date); how the debtor should do it (put a check or money order in the mail or bring it into the office).

You can make it easier for the debtor to respond by enclosing a return envelope. But give the debtor a chance to bring up any question or problem he or she has with making the payment, by reminding the debtor to speak up now. For example, you might close with something like, "We'll assume you agree this amount is due and will look forward to payment on June 15, unless we hear from you to the contrary."

Using Telephone Techniques That Work

You can use the telephone at any stage in the collection process in place of letters or to supplement the letters you send. Usually, though, the telephone works best when you want to: notify or remind a friend that a debt is due before you start sending letters (unless your friend lives some distance away); follow up after you have sent out a notification, reminder, or appeals letter that hasn't worked; or follow up after a debtor has broken a promise made to you in a previous call or letter.

As with letters, you should follow a general formula for making an effective collections contact but adapt your phone approach to your personal style. When you start making calls, have a general outline or script of what you are going to say in mind so you can cover all points. Yet be flexible to respond to what the debtor says. It also helps to have some responses already prepared to the objections or excuses the debtor is likely to make.

Once you make a number of these calls, you'll find the responses commonly fall into a pattern; you can easily start building a file of stock answers.

Divide your call into several phases, giving your statement, proposal, and reasons, then asking for action. In the phone call the debtor can raise questions and objections, and you have to answer these successfully before you can get the action you want.

Be sure to tell the debtor about the situation. State why the debtor should pay the amount due in full, today. Then listen as the debtor tells you why he or she will not or cannot pay everything. This response is often just an excuse. Your job is to come back with a rebuttal that gets around the response. This response-rebuttal phase may continue for a while, as the debtor raises additional points that require rebuttal, but after you finish answering, seek action by initiating an agreement with the debtor--then ask him or her to act based on that agreement.

Keep your call brief and to the point. Even with a friend or business associate, avoid getting chatty. Instead, zero in on the reason for your call as soon as possible and keep your call to only a few minutes. You are making a business sales call and you want to build up to your close quickly.

Speak with authority and firmness, though you should balance this by being friendly and supportive if the debtor is cooperative. You don't want to sound angry or hostile.

Make it clear that the situation is serious and there is some urgency. Initially, you can sound more casual. Then, as time goes on and the debtor doesn't pay, step up your intimations of urgency and concern.

Treat the debtor with diplomacy and respect. Unless you are good friends or already on a first-name basis, use the debtor's surname. It's easier to maintain the necessary distance and objectivity when you avoid first names, for using them creates a false intimacy and may also make the debtor feel you are being condescending and treating him or her like a child.

Choose your words carefully. Just as in writing letters, you should stay with terms such as "past due" instead of "you're delinquent." Use courtesy and tact, especially at first, to preserve the debtor's good will. Later, if the debtor doesn't pay and you no longer care much about good will, you should continue to relate to the debtor in a dignified manner. You don't want to end up slinging insults and names. Succumbing to the temptation to use unprofessional language (e.g., "deadbeat," "lowlife," "cheat") will only succeed in making the debtor angry and even less likely to pay.

Try to present your case from the debtor's point of view. Why should he or she want to pay? Use motivating reasons. As in writing letters, try to avoid sentences beginning with "I," "we," "my," or "our." If you appear concerned about the debtor, you will make him or her more receptive to working with you.

Organizing Your Call

The collection call has five phases: identifying the debtor and yourself; making an opening statement in which you summarize the debt and ask the debtor for payment; pausing to give the debtor a chance to respond; answering questions and objections, and presenting a solution or payment plan; and, finally, closing the agreement.

Identifying the Debtor and Yourself

Before you start talking about a debt, you have to identify the debtor. Unless you already know the debtor, this identification process can be tricky. You have to be certain you are talking to the debtor and not to anyone else. Remember, you aren't supposed to talk to other people about the debt, or you run into the problem of defaming the debtor's character.

The first step in a collection call, then, is talking to the debtor directly. Sometimes you have to overcome assorted obstacles to doing this, such as secretaries and assistants or debtors who don't want to identify themselves. You may have to think of various ploys to get through. As an individual you have more freedom to be creative, since bill collectors are expressly prohibited from being deceptive.

Here are some effective strategies.

If the person answering fits the description of the debtor, start off your conversation by saying, "Is this (debtor's name)?" rather than "May I speak to (debtor's name)?" This way you come off with more authority, and if you get the debtor, he or she is likely to say "Yes," not "Who's this?"

If you get a secretary or assistant, make your call sound urgent. Some inventive creditors will say that theirs is a long-distance call. For example, "This is long distance calling for Mr./Ms. (debtor's name). Can you please connect us?" While this approach is novel, it does border on misrepresentation.

If a secretary or assistant questions what the call is about, you might imply that you are a close friend or business associate and that he or she knows why you are calling. For example: "This is (your name). He'll know what this is about."

Alternatively, you can stress the urgency of the call and emphasize that it's a personal matter that you can't talk about with anyone else. Say firmly, "It's a personal matter. I need to speak to him directly myself; I'm not at liberty to discuss this with anyone else."

If you can't reach the debtor, avoid leaving a message. If possible, find out when the person will be in so you can call again and give a logical reason why he or she can't call you back. For example, "It's really important that I reach him directly about an urgent matter, and he won't be able to call me back, because I'm calling from the field. But if you can tell me when he'll be in, I'll call back then." Then call exactly when you have been asked to call. You'll increase your chances of reaching the debtor if you make the call, and you'll be prepared with what to say, instead of answering the phone sometime and finding the debtor on the line.

However you do it, once you have the debtor on the line, immediately introduce yourself, using your first and last name, and the company you are representing. ("Hello. This is John Smith of ABC Company.")

Making an Opening Statement

As soon as you identify yourself to the debtor, make your opening statement summarizing the situation. Like the opening line of a letter, this statement should be concise and to the point so you immediately have the debtor's attention and interest.

This opening is usually the time to state how much money is due and how long it has been owing. However, if you are calling to follow up on a letter or previous call in which the debtor made a promise not yet kept, you can refer to that and state that you have still not received the money. For example, depending on the situation, your statement might go something like this:

> "I'm calling about the $300 balance on your stereo equipment, which is still overdue after 3 months."

> "We haven't received our payment of $300 after sending you a letter about it last week."

> "You promised you would be sending us $300 when we spoke on the phone last week, but it hasn't arrived yet as scheduled."

Briefly add a proposal for action and underline the urgency of that action by stressing that the debtor must do it today, possibly giving a reason why quick action is necessary. Be firm when you say this; depending on how long the problem has been going on, consider using a "good guy" or "tough guy" approach. For example:

> (Good guy approach:) "We'd like to get this matter settled quickly so we can keep you as a valued customer and not turn off your credit. So please get your check in the mail before noon today."

> (Tough guy approach:) "We're going to have to take some legal action on this matter, if we don't get payment promptly. I'm sure you want to keep your good credit record. So we'll need your

check in the mail before noon today."

Pausing for the Debtor's Response

Once you've made your statement, be quiet; let the debtor respond. This is a psychological technique used by bill collectors to transfer the burden of giving an explanation or reason for nonpayment to the debtor.

You may feel uncomfortable with the silence. But let it continue, so the debtor knows it's up to him or her to say something. At most, you might say something like "Well?" Leave it up to the debtor to respond.

At this point, if the debtor is honest and feels responsible for the debt, he or she will typically agree to pay all or some of the money or will offer a reason for not paying it. However, the debtor may come up with some excuse to put you off.

Addressing Questions and Objections—
and Discussing Payment Arrangements

You may not always be able to determine if the debtor is responding honestly or just making up an excuse; but initially, go on the assumption that the debtor is being honest. Then if the debtor continues to give you reasons for nonpayment or breaks promises to pay, you can start assuming the debtor is trying to get out of paying and respond accordingly.

If you believe the debtor is being honest, this is the time to ask if there is some problem behind his or her failure to pay the debt and to discuss any problems. If the debtor raises questions or objections, deal with them as if they are valid issues and concerns. If you respond to the debtor satisfactorily, he or she is likely to pay. Otherwise, he or she will probably continue to resist.

On the other hand, if you feel the debtor is just giving excuses, this is the time to call the debtor on these and get tough.

Have a possible payment plan in mind in case the debtor can't pay everything all at once. For example, you might have devised an arrangement that calls for a partial payment once a week, bi-weekly, or monthly until the balance is paid off. Then, if appropriate, offer this plan during the conversation. But first, do what you can to get the whole amount.

During this phase of the conversation, you are often acting like a salesperson and making appeals to the debtor. If the debtor seems honest, you can use the higher appeals to feelings of honor, belonging, pride, and self-respect. If you sense the debtor is not being straight with you, use the more basic lower level appeals to the debtor's self-interest in seeking security, safety, freedom from worry, and staying out of trouble.

There are basically two types of objections the debtor may raise. Assuming they are valid concerns, not just false excuses, you should use the following overall strategy. (We'll get into specific approaches in the next part of this book.)

Objections to the debt in whole or in part. In this case, your job is to clarify what those objections are and get agreement on areas where there is no objection. If the objections are minor, you can work out compromises; if they are serious, you will probably need to gather more facts in order to resolve the problem.

Objections to the payment plan you propose. Here, the objections are likely to have to do with the amount or frequency of each payment. Work on developing a program the debtor can agree to, yet one that isn't extended so long you feel the debtor is evading the debt.

Closing

Finally, after you have discussed the debt, offered your proposal, and dealt with any questions and objections, it is time to firm up the agreement and close the deal. At this point, you summarize what you and the debtor have agreed and indicate what action the debtor is going to take next. For example, you might say something like the following:

> "Okay, let's review what we agreed on, so we both have every-thing straight. We are agreed that the total debt owing is $1,000 and that you will be sending me a payment of $100 every month, starting June 15. You'll be putting your first payment in the mail today so I'll receive it by June 17th. You'll also come over on the 19th to write up an agreement with me stating what we have agreed today."

Follow-Up

After your phone conversation, write down what you and the debtor agreed to do and follow-up to make sure the debtor keeps any promises. If the debtor doesn't, which often happens, you'll need to stay on top of the situation and call or write again to remind the debtor and increase the intensity of your appeal. With many debtors, this follow-up is crucial. It can mean the difference between the debtor putting your debt on the back burner or your getting paid!

CHAPTER 11:
Early Contacts with the Debtor

Once the loan or credit you have extended becomes overdue, the first stage of the collection process begins. Usually, creditors allow a few days as a grace period, on the assumption that the payment is on its way by mail. But then they begin the process of notifying and reminding the debtor.

The assumption at this stage is that the debtor has overlooked paying the debt and, once notified or reminded, will pay. Thus, the first notification is typically very gentle, with each reminder getting a little stronger. The emphasis is on treating the debtor as a well-intentioned, responsible person or company and on maintaining good will.

Commonly, this stage lasts about 30 days, and creditors generally use notes, letters, or notices stamped on bills to let the debtor know the account is overdue, though some may phone. Commonly, too, creditors make up to two or three contacts at this stage before stepping up the pressure by moving on to stage two.

However, some creditors don't believe in extending this process. After one or two contacts without getting paid, they move directly to the appeals or final demand stage and plan to take the whole matter quickly to court if they must.

There is no single correct formula. Use the approach that best fits your personal style and seems best suited to the particular situation and debtor.

The First Notification

When you first discover that a bill or loan is overdue, there are several notification strategies. Whichever you use, you should clearly indicate the amount due. If the debtor has any question or dispute about the balance owing, he or she will let you know.

If you are using a monthly statement or billing system, send a duplicate copy of the unpaid statement or invoice to the customer, and stamp it PAST DUE! Or use this popular variation: PAST DUE! PLEASE SEND CHECK BY RETURN MAIL. The advantage of this method in some situations is that it is impersonal, so the debtor won't feel any personal slight.

If the statement or bill is only a few days overdue, you might write a few brief words on the invoice such as "JUST DUE" or "PLEASE," or

"URGENT." Again, the advantage is the impersonal touch, although you can use handwriting to give your statement a more personal flavor, and you can adapt your comment to specific situations.

For a little more personal touch, consider combining a stamped or handwritten notice with a brief note. This works well if you already know the debtor. For example, to a business owner you have previously met, you might write something like: "Hi, Joe. This probably fell through the cracks. Can you take care of it?"

You might also consider sending out a brief letter announcing that the bill is due. Some creditors use a form letter and fill in the amount; others type out new copy each time. For instance:

Dear Ms. Smith:
Your bill for $100 was due on June 15 and is now ten days overdue. Can you please send your check by return mail? Thanks for your cooperation.
Sincerely,

You might decide to make a phone call to notify the debtor. This usually works best if you are calling a small company, where you speak personally to the owner; a quick comment about the debt is all you need. For instance: "I just wanted to call to let you know your bill (loan) for $100 is overdue by a few days. Could you please send in your payment?"

Since it's more cost effective, most creditors use some variation on the stamped notice or brief letter, rather than trying to call. But if you have only a few overdue accounts or know the people involved, you may prefer the personal touch. Use what works for you.

Sending Out Reminders

After your first notification, wait about ten to fifteen days to see if you get paid. If not, it's time to send out reminders. Most creditors still use a letter or other written notice at this stage (though some phone) indicating the balance due and any account number.

As with the notification, at this stage the assumption is still that the debtor has forgotten about the bill, accepts the balance, and will pay it once reminded. Accordingly, your communications about the bill should still be routine, and there is no need yet to initiate a discussion about payment or make appeals to the debtor. If the debtor has any quibble with the amount, it's his or her responsibility to raise that objection.

While some creditors send up to six or seven reminders, others may send only one or two to speed up the collection process. A good reason for sending only a few reminders is that if these don't work, it's likely there is some problem behind the person's failure to pay (generally a dispute or cash flow problem), and often debtors don't volunteer these explanations. They simply continue to ignore the reminders until the creditor raises the issue.

Types of Reminders

There are three written types of reminders in addition to the option of a follow-up phone call. In each, you quickly describe the situation or problem (payment is overdue), suggest that the debtor probably overlooked this, propose what the debtor should do (pay the bill), and ask for action now (send in your check). Some creditors add a brief tag line that the debtor should excuse the reminder if he or she has already sent in the payment. But that's not necessary. If the debtor has sent in a recent payment, he or she will be aware your correspondence has probably crossed in the mail.

The four reminders are: the personal letter; the impersonal form letter; the stamped reminder or printed sticker; and the reminder phone call.

The Personal Letter

This is probably the most effective reminder because it shows you have singled out the account or bill for personal attention.

Keep the letter brief and to the point; suggest that the debtor probably forgot about the bill, and point out that that's why you're sending a personal reminder to make payment. If it's a friend or business associate you know well, you might even include a dash of humor (such as a pouting face with the word "please" underneath). A good strategy at this point is to emphasize the routineness of the request by saying that you need the payment to get your books in order at the end of the month, or that you have to update your records. Then, if you have to get tough later, you can always blame your accountant to preserve good will as long as possible.

If you have a lot of these letters, you can cut down on your costs by using a computer. Feed in a basic letter, insert the debtor's name, amount, date due, and account number, if any, in the appropriate places, and the letter comes out looking like a personal letter.

Some examples follow.

Dear Mr. Smith:

Probably you overlooked this, but your bill for $300 from June is still overdue. We sent you a notice about this 10 days ago.

Can you please send in your check so we can close our books on this matter? Or if your check is already in the mail, please excuse this notice.

Sincerely,

Hi Chuck:

Old Simon Legree is on the rampage again.

But seriously, I still haven't gotten the $300 you promised to pay me back on my loan, though I sent you a notice two weeks ago to let you know payment was overdue.

So please send along your check. Then my accountant can balance my books.

Sincerely,

Another good technique for personal letters is to give the debtor a way to save face by suggesting that you understand he or she is busy and probably didn't have time to send payment. Also, you can make it more convenient for the debtor to send in the money by enclosing an envelope.

Dear Ms. Allen:

You're usually very busy, and that's probably why you have forgotten to pay us the $300 overdue on your account.

To make it easy for you to take care of this, I've enclosed a self-addressed envelope. Won't you please send in your check today, so we can keep your account up to date?

Sincerely,

Another approach that works well when you know or have regular business dealings with the debtor is to make your letter even more personal by adding a handwritten note from you or someone the debtor knows. For example, before he sends out reminders to customers, one business owner has the salesperson handling the account write a casual note on the bottom of the letter saying something like, "Hi Joe; hope you'll be sending in your check soon."

The Impersonal Form Letter

This is a variation of the personal letter; it says much the same thing. In essence, it states that this is a reminder: the account is overdue, please send in payment. But it is obviously a form letter; the letter is designed so that you can fill in the blanks with the correct amount.

With some debtors using a form letter is an advantage, because they don't have to take your requests for payment personally: your billing seems to be coming from your accounting department. As a result, in some situations impersonal billing can help a debtor save face. Say you have a business relationship with a friend who is having cash flow problems, and is a little slow paying. You can preserve your friendship without seeming to dun him yourself, unless things get serious.

A typical form letter might look something like the one reproduced below.

> Dear _____:
> Here's a friendly reminder to let you know your account # _____ for $_____ is now overdue.
> You may have overlooked our previous notice to you, so here's a second notice for your convenience.
> Can you please put your check in the mail today?
> Sincerely

The Stamped Reminder of Printed Sticker

Another approach is to send the debtor the original bill with another "past due" notification stamp. But in contrast to the initial notification, this notice is a little more urgent, and the repetition serves as a follow-up reminder. For example, the stamp might announce something like:

> PAST DUE!
> PLEASE REMIT TODAY!

Or it might go into more detail, such as this stamp:

> A FRIENDLY REMINDER:
> YOUR ACCOUNT IS OVERDUE.
> WE'VE BEEN EXPECTING YOUR CHECK.
> WON'T YOU PLEASE SEND IT TODAY?

You can obtain preprinted stamps in a stationery supply store or nave them made with your own message.

You can also purchase preprinted stickers--or create your own. Some examples follow.

> WE DIDN'T GET YOUR EXPECTED PAYMENT LAST MONTH. CAN YOU PLEASE SEND IT TODAY?

YOUR ACCOUNT IS OVERDUE
AND WE'RE WAITING TO HEAR FROM YOU
WITH YOUR CHECK!

The Reminder Phone Call

A reminder phone call can be used for two major purposes. It can be employed as an immediate follow-up to your initial notification if you have extended credit to a friend and feel a more personal touch is needed, or if the amount due is particularly large and you seek quick action. In addition, it can act as an interim reminder between sending reminder letters or statements.

Many creditors stay away from phone calls until things get serious, because phone calls can be time consuming (particularly when you have difficulty getting the debtor to come to the phone or call back). Moreover, if the debtor lives or works out of the area, the costs of phoning can mount up, and a small debt is probably not worth a call.

But if the amount due is large, or you suddenly become concerned about the debtor's ability to pay as a result of recent developments (for example, the business loses a big customer or your friend gets fired from a job), by all means, call. You may need to take action fast to collect anything, and in this case, the usual, gradual, step-up-the-pressure approach to collections will move too slowly.

Additional Reminders

If your first reminder doesn't work, the next usual step is increasing the pressure on the debtor with any of the following strategies, or perhaps a combination of them.

Consider using a more intense personal letter or series of increasingly intense letters; try a personal phone call or visit; or send a mailgram or telegram showing you mean business.

At this point, you don't want to send out any more impersonal form letters or reminders, since they haven't been effective. Instead, you have to start personalizing and/or intensifying the process.

Sending Out More Intense Personal Letters

Some creditors use a series of reminder letters of increasing urgency. These are still polite and courteous, written on the assumption the debtor is basically an honorable person, who only needs to be prodded. These reminders become increasingly firm and more insistent as the emphasis shifts from gently prodding to urging the debtor to take care of the matter immediately and send in the money that's due.

The reminder letter has another important function: it helps establish the validity of the debt in case the debtor should subsequently dispute it. The letter has this power because if the debt isn't valid, the debtor should not ignore the letter but should call the debt into question. If he or she doesn't, this helps support your case.

My own feeling is that one or at most two reminders are enough. Unless the debtor is genuinely dense, he or she knows you are asking for the money. Repeated reminders will only prolong the process, and you need to find out from the debtor the reason he or she has still not paid.

Some Examples of Follow-Up Personal Letters

One type of polite and courteous reminder letter tells the debtor you are sending another reminder because he or she hasn't responded to a previous reminder and may have misplaced the earlier bill. This letter may also urge the debtor to act now to avoid further reminders. Here are two letters that are still reminders, although the second is a little more firm and insistent than the first:

> Dear Ms. Wyatt:
> This is a second reminder about the $100 you owe us for the books we sent you in June.
> You can avoid us bothering you with any more reminders by sending in your check today.
> Sincerely,

> Dear Ms. Wyatt:
> You have not responded to our previous statement and notices about the $100 due for the books we sent you in June. Since we know you are busy and may have easily misplaced or overlooked our bill, we're sending you this last reminder.
> So, please, since this bill has been unpaid for two months, let's get this matter settled now. Please send in your check today.
> Sincerely,

Another strategy for a follow-up letter is to combine a reminder with a statement of what you, the creditor, have done to help the debtor and to emphasize that you believe you have done everything to carry out your part of the agreement. You might also mention your hope to continue to work together for mutual benefit, implying that this will end if the debtor doesn't pay. Finally, you might remind the debtor he or she can always phone if there is any problem.

PAST DUE BALANCE: ($____.__)
Dear Mr./Ms._____:
Why have you not yet responded to our several friendly reminders of your past due balance?

We shipped the merchandise that you ordered. Didn't you receive it? Is there a problem with the bill?

The outstanding balance has been overdue for some time. Please send payment today to clear the account.

If there is a problem, please call us today. We want to help you clear your account as soon as possible.

Very truly yours,

Making Follow-Up Calls

While many creditors use this two-step reminder approach with personal letters, some combine a reminder letter with a follow-up phone call, or reverse the process and call first. If that doesn't work, they send a letter 10 to 15 days later.

Whenever you call, you should say much the same thing as you would in a letter. Keep it casual and polite, though firm.

If your call is a follow-up to your first notification, then your tone should be relatively supportive and gentle. But if you've already sent out one reminder, then sound more urgent and intense.

(A Follow-Up Call After a Notification Letter:)
Hello...This is _____. I just wanted to be sure you got our letter notifying you that your account for $200 is overdue. Well, this is just another friendly reminder to ask you to send in your check, so we can close our books on this matter.

(A Follow-Up Call After a Previous Reminder Letter:)
Hello...This is _____. I'm surprised we didn't hear from you, since we've sent you two letters about your account. The current balance of $200 has been overdue for about two months, and I wanted to remind you about this matter. We certainly value you as a customer, and would like to get your account up to date. So won't you please send in your payment today?

Sending Mailgrams or Telegrams

Some creditors follow the first or second reminder letter with a telegram or mailgram. The advantage of this type of reminder is that it conveys more urgency than a personal letter, and it's particularly good if a substantial amount of money is at stake (say, over $200; on small amounts a telegram reminder may seem like overkill and it may not be cost effective to send one out).

If you use a telegram, keep it short and snappy, since people expect this when they get a telegram. Brevity conveys urgency. For example, you might say something like:

A SECOND REMINDER:
YOUR ACCOUNT FOR $675 IS LONG OVERDUE. PLEASE SEND IN YOUR PAYMENT IMMEDIATELY SO THAT WE CAN CLEAR THIS PAST DUE BALANCE.

Alternatively, you can send out a longer mailgram. This service is provided by Western Union and enables you to send a full-length collection letter for the price of an ordinary telegram. You include what you might say in an ordinary reminder letter. But the letter is transmitted by wire and comes in an envelope like a telegram, so it appears more urgent than an ordinary letter.

Moving On

In sum, the notification/reminder phase is designed to prod the debtor to pay on the assumption that he or she can and will. However, if, after several reminders, you still haven't been paid, it's time to up the ante and start using psychological appeals to motivate the debtor to pay. If the reminders haven't worked--it's time to bring out the "stick" or the "carrots."

CHAPTER 12:
Appeals that
Motivate the Debtor

After the debtor has ignored your reminders to pay for a month or two, you have to change your assumption that the debtor has merely overlooked or forgotten the debt. You know he or she knows about it. Now you have to assume there is some problem, and you must overcome it to get paid. Much as a salesperson persuades a customer to act, you must appeal to the debtor, overcome any objections, and convince him or her to pay.

You'll encounter three basic problems, and dozens of variations on each theme.

(1) The debtor acknowledges the debt but claims he or she hasn't got enough money to pay. (Your task, accordingly is to work with the debtor to a) help him or her get the money, b) realize there are resources of which he or she may not be aware, c) put a higher priority on paying you, or d) work out a payment arrangement to pay you over time.)

(2) The debtor honestly disputes the debt and won't pay until the dispute is resolved. (Now your task is to work out a solution to the debt and, if possible, get payment for the undisputed amount while you work out a solution for the rest.)

(3) The debtor does not want to pay and may claim a lack of money or a dispute. However, the debtor is really a deadbeat who has no intention of paying if he or she can evade the debt. (Your job now is to get through any smokescreens the debtor puts up, show you mean business, and appeal to the debtor's self-interest or to a fear of what will happen if the debt isn't paid.)

A key part of the appeals process is finding out exactly what is wrong and why, so you can appropriately confront the problem and determine the best way to solve it. You must become something of a problem-solver and psychologist to figure out the best way to write, call, or meet with the debtor to resolve the problem.

Some creditors use letters as much as possible in this phase, since it generally takes less time and costs less to follow up in writing, particularly if the debtor lives or works far away. But frequently you have to talk to the debtor personally to work things out. Adapt your approach to the circumstances and size of the debt.

Because many issues can arise at this point, the appeals phase may last longer than any other part of the collection process (with the notable exception of going to court and trying to collect at the end). Commonly, this phase starts after a month of reminders and lasts about 30 to 60 days, although in some cases it can drag on for many months, even a year or more, if the debtor is particularly good at coming up with excuses and the creditor is especially patient.

But normally, you should plan on keeping the process as short as possible. Get to the heart of the problem quickly, appeal to the debtor with increasing firmness, and work on finding a solution that is mutually agreeable to you and the debtor--unless you conclude the debtor is a deadbeat. If the debtor still doesn't pay, move quickly into the final demand stage. Lastly, take whatever action you have threatened.

By moving quickly, you'll avoid the common trap of many creditors: getting stuck in an endless appeals process. When you know how to target your appeals appropriately, and you overcome any problems standing in the way of payment, you'll usually get your money from a debtor who is basically honest. If you don't get paid, why waste time treading water with deadbeats?   Catch a wave and get tough.

Initiating the Appeals Process

You can initiate the appeals process in several ways: sending out a letter with one or more appeals; calling up the debtor to find out what the problem is, so you can direct your appeal accordingly; or asking the debtor to meet with you personally to discuss the matter.

You can call the debtor to set up an appointment; or, if you see each other regularly (as friends or business associates), set up a meeting then.

Many creditors prefer to arrange a meeting about the debt far in advance, so the debtor can come to the meeting prepared to discuss the debt and can bring along any relevant records or correspondence if a dispute occurs. You might ask a person you see regularly, "When's a good time to get together to discuss our financial arrangement?   Since this has been going on for a while, I thought it might be a good idea to sit down and discuss it, in case there are some problems we need to work out."

Whether it's better to start off the appeals process with a letter, phone call, or personal meeting depends on your situation. Here are some guidelines to keep in mind.

The Letter. This is probably the all around best approach for routine business matters. The first letter is typically fairly warm, polite, and respectful, since you still hope to keep the customer or client's good will. But now you are appealing to the debtor to pay and asking him or her to advise you if there is any problem. Initially, it's best to state your appeal in a general way, since until you talk to the debtor and find out why he or she hasn't paid, you won't be sure how to proceed. The letter has several advantages. First, it is a fairly low-cost and diplomatic way to motivate the debtor and uncover any problems. Secondly, if the matter should end up in court, you have another document to support your claims.

With debtors you know personally, the objectivity of the letter can sometimes be an advantage in keeping your relationship on a friendly footing. You can make it appear that you're not directly bugging someone to pay--it's your office or accountant who's doing it. However, some friends and associates might be put off by the objectivity; they would prefer to hear about any problems directly from you. Use your own judgment.

The Phone Call. This is a common approach when a debt involves a friend or close business associate. If you are used to communicating regularly by phone, it might make sense to continue to do so and to get to the heart of the problem. The call is also good with local people or companies who are relatively easy to reach by phone. The advantage of using the phone is that you don't have to appeal in broad generalities, as is common in a first appeals letter. Instead, you can ask the debtor directly for a reason for nonpayment and immediately seek to work out a solution. The disadvantage is that a verbal discussion can sometimes leave more room for misunderstanding. Verbal agreements are also less compelling in court. If you already have a written agreement, or if you follow up your call with a letter reconfirming what you have both said, you can avoid building on misunderstandings. Furthermore, your summary letter, if not contradicted by the debtor, will carry some weight in court.

The Personal Meeting. This is ideal if the debt is a substantial amount and involves someone in the area with whom you have an ongoing business relationship or friendship. If you don't already have a written agreement, the personal meeting is an opportunity to extract a promissory note reaffirming the debt and the debtor's intention to pay. With a large amount, it's probably best to go to the debtor's home or office yourself so you can check out the debtor's situation first hand. If the business is in trouble, you'll be able to tell when you walk through the plant or office. Perhaps you see many machines idle or desks empty; that might suggest a recent layoff.

After your first appeals letter, call, or meeting, follow up if the debtor doesn't follow through as agreed. Some creditors, particularly if the debt is large and not disputed, now move immediately to the final demand stage. Others may try a few more appeals.

Since circumstances vary so widely (the size of the debt, the debtor's reasons for nonpayment, your assessment of the debtor's financial circumstances and intention to pay, your relationship to the debtor, your desire to continue working with the debtor, and your own style) you should use your own judgment on the best approach for you.

In any event, if the debtor has responded to your first appeal with a promise and breaks it, follow up as soon as this happens to show you're right on top of things. Otherwise, follow up about 10 to 15 days after your first appeal. Again, depending on your own situation, choose the letter, phone, or meeting approach.

While some creditors use a series of letters or phone calls, you might consider varying the mix. For example, if your first letter doesn't produce results, try the phone. If you have worked out an agreement on the phone and the debtor doesn't fulfill this, mention it in a follow-up letter. Use letters or calls to follow up after a meeting, or set up a meeting if your letters or calls don't work.

A common arrangement is to make two or, at most, three appeals before going on to the final demand. Most honest debtors who value their reputation or a continued relationship with you will pay at this point. With the others, I recommend getting tough: it's the old story of the squeaky wheel getting the grease. At one time I spent weeks trying to be conciliatory with nearly a dozen debtors, who dragged out the process endlessly with one excuse after another. Meanwhile, there were other creditors they paid. When I finally got tough and filed suit, a few of them suddenly came up with the cash or were willing to sit down and resolve a dispute after evading my calls and letters for months.

So use the appeals process for a limited time (I recommend for two months at most) and don't get stuck by being too nice and understanding. If the debtor doesn't respond after a reasonable time, it's time to get tough.

The Basic Steps of Motivating the Debtor

The appeals process is much like selling. However, you're not selling a product or service. Rather, you're selling the debtor on the belief that it's in his or her best interest to pay the debt.

The five basic principles of selling have been widely noted in books on sales techniques. These steps, modified a little to suit your purposes as a creditor, are outlined below.

(1) Attracting the debtor's attention.

(2) Building the debtor's interest in what you have to say.

(3) Developing the debtor's conviction that the situation is serious and must be resolved immediately.

(4) Encouraging the debtor's desire to pay.

(5) Making the close and getting the debtor to make a payment.

Attracting the Debtor's Attention

You want the debtor to listen to what you have to say, so start off your letter, phone call, or meeting with something interesting or attention-getting. ("You don't want to lose your excellent credit rating with our store, do you?")

Questions or strong statements are good "grabbers." You want to avoid rambling introductions like: "In reviewing our records, it has come to our attention that..." When you call, don't sound unsure of yourself or take too long to make an introduction. Get right to the point to get the debtor's attention.

Your initial approach is extremely important. You have between four and ten seconds to make your first impression and get the person's attention. In this short time, the person decides if he or she wants to listen to what you say next and develops a mental set about how to receive this information.

When you make the right approach, the person is likely to be receptive, or, at least willing to consider seriously what you have to say. When your approach is wrong, the person will tune you out or fail to consider what you are saying very important. To continue any communication effectively, you then have to struggle to reverse that first impression.

Just as in sales, it is critical to gain the right kind of attention from the beginning in collecting a debt.

Building the Debtor's Interest in What You Say

Face it. In collecting a bill you are not "selling" a very popular product or service. But you still have to build the debtor's interest by stressing the benefits he or she will receive in paying your bill.

So don't simply restate how much is due. The debtor probably knows that very well already after getting your reminders. Instead, give reasons why the debtor will benefit. This process is much like explaining the advantages a buyer will gain from a product or service, instead of explaining how the product works and why. All good salespeople will agree on the importance of stressing benefits (how the prospect will be better off after a decision to buy) rather than product features (the specifics of how that benefit is delivered). It's exactly the same when you try to collect.

For example, say something like, "You'll be able to clear up this credit rating problem in just a few minutes, if we can settle your overdue bill of $200." This represents a much more productive approach than something like, "We've already sent you several reminders about the $200 you owe and you still owe it."

To be effective in collecting, as in sales, you need to find out about the person's motives and interests, so you can direct your appeals accordingly. Thus, when you call or meet with the debtor, ask questions and listen to find out what he or she wants. Or in a letter, urge the debtor to phone or write you about any problems. Not only will the information you get be crucial for your appeals strategy, but letting the debtor react is valuable because it gets him or her involved in resolving the collection problem. The debtor will feel the two of you are working together, not escalating a "me against you" situation.

Developing the Debtor Conviction that the Situation is Serious and Must be Resolved Immediately

After you've gotten attention and interest, you want to convince the debtor that you are worth listening to, and that your message is an important one requiring a positive response very soon. (This is like convincing a prospect you have a valuable product and selling yourself along with the product.)

Your first impression starts the process. During the rest of your presentation, continue to back that up.

When you call, sound forceful and assertive. When you send a letter, make sure it's carefully typed on an impressive letterhead. If you have a personal meeting, dress in a stylish, businesslike way to show that you consider this a serious matter. Even if you are appealing to a friend, a good appearance helps to reinforce your message.

Besides making a good first impression, convey to the debtor your own conviction that the debtor will and should pay, just as if you were a salesperson promoting a product you believe in. To be convincing, you must appear confident, and to appear this way, you must believe in your ability to collect and the debtor's ability to pay. Then, when you write or talk to the debtor, the style or tone of your communication will convey this message.

Encouraging the Debtor's Desire to Pay

To spark desire, you need to combine interest and conviction with an appeal to the emotions. It's just like selling a product. You can make a person interested in listening or convince him or her that what you say has merit by appealing to his or her intellect. But to make a person truly desire something (including wanting to pay a debt) you have to engage the emotions, too.

This is the purpose of using the major appeals. You can make your appeals even more powerful by the language you use when you talk or write to the debtor.

Just as a salesperson paints an attractive picture of a product so that the prospect can almost see, taste, smell, or otherwise experience possessing it, you can sell someone on paying a debt. For example, mention the specific disadvantages a person might experience in losing his or her credit with you so that the debtor feels a sense of loss. ("We'll be having a special sale for our customers who have good credit next week, and you'll be able to save 50-60% on top-brand products. If we can get your overdue balance resolved by then, you'll be able to take advantage of this sale.")

Like a salesperson, you can also appeal to the debtor's feeling of self-importance or self-image. ("I know you value your reputation as a successful businessman in your industry...")

Reaching "Yes"

The final step in a collections contact is making the close. Here, just as in sales, you ask the person to take action. When you write a letter, you assume the person has been convinced and is ready to act at the end. But if you are talking to the debtor, you have to be sensitive about when he or she is ready to act. You must watch for the appropriate "buy" signals indicating the person has been sold by what you have said. Accordingly, when the debtor seems ready to respond (for example, when you hear comments like, "Yeah, I understand I better get that debt paid off now," or "You're right. I sure wouldn't want to lose my credit with you"), it's time to close by asking for some action.

As in sales, you can ask for this action directly. "Why don't we close this matter now by having you pay me $100 now? Then we'll write up a promissory note stating you will pay me $100 each month for the next three months."

For another type of close, do as many salespeople do: assume the person has already agreed to what you are selling or stating and act on that basis. This is what is called the "assumptive close." For example, you pull out an agreement form and say, "Okay. Would you prefer to give me the first payment in cash or write a check? Just sign here to confirm our agreement."

The Major Appeals

When the debtor owes money and believes he or she owes at least part of the debt, appeals to his or her honor, pride, self-interest, and other motivators can be effective. Different approaches are needed when the debtor disputes the debt or is intentionally trying to avoid it.

Assuming the debtor accepts the validity of the debt, your object is to find ways to get the debtor to pay. Claims of no money are no excuse.

You've got to motivate the debtor to find the money. And if the debtor has other debts competing for attention, which many do, you're in a competitive sales situation. You've got to work even harder to motivate the debtor to pay you, not someone else.

There are five basic motivators or appeals. Salespeople use them to promote attention, interest, conviction, desire, and to close a sale. You'll find them similarly effective in trying to collect.

These five major appeals are directed to the following key needs of the debtor: physical needs for self-preservation and protection; security needs for comfort and ease; social needs for belonging, friendship, affection and love; ego needs for self-esteem, reputation, status, recognition, pride, respect, self-confidence, achievement or independence; and self-fulfillment needs for realizing one's potential, being creative, and achieving financial success.

Key motivators can be viewed as a hierarchy, in that a person seeks to satisfy a lower-order need first (a view advanced by the psychologist Abraham Maslow). As a person fulfills a lower need, he or she becomes interested in satisfying a higher one.

The flip side of the coin is that each need is associated with a concern or fear of not achieving that need (a fact especially relevant to collection from debtors). As a collector, you typically have to emphasize the negative or loss side of the appeal to make the debtor feel anxious or nervous. These five major appeals are summarized below from this perspective.

Difficulties with self-preservation and protection. (No, this doesn't mean the Mafia will attack; the problem can be something quite legal, like loss of a home or a car.)

Discomfort and everyday difficulties. (For example, more annoying phone calls and letters; loss of a secured property like a TV or stereo; difficulty in getting credit or loss of a good credit rating.)

Loneliness; lack of love and affection. (Here, statements highlighting the loss might be appropriate. "Nobody likes someone who doesn't meet obligations." "If you lose your credit, you won't be able to keep up with your crowd.")

Shame; dishonor. (The implication here is that it's shameful or dishonorable not to pay debts; upstanding, respectable members of the community make a commitment to pay and do.)

A failure in achieving personal or business goals. ("You won't have credit when you need it for your business." "You may lose out on future business deals if you can't pay a debt now.")

Conversely, when the debtor pays, he or she gains the corresponding advantages: security, comfort, belonging, recognition, or self-fulfillment.

Deciding What Appeals to Use

You can decide on the best appeal or appeals based on the information you have, or learn about the debtor as you seek to collect. You can use data on the debtor's income level, lifestyle, and community involvement, and on the nature of debt (purchase, business loan, or personal loan) to give you clues. If you talk to the debtor, ask questions to gain more information If the debtor responds to you with a letter, review it carefully.

In choosing an appeal, you are like a salesperson sizing up the prospect or an ad copywriter trying to find the right approach to make the customer buy. Successful salespeople learn to listen and probe to find out what motivates a customer: that person's so-called "hot button." When you speak to the debtor, you should do the same.

In advertising, copywriters use a variety of themes in an ad campaign to motivate action, and you might think of writing a series of appeals letters that way. If one hot button doesn't work, try another, each time stepping up the pressure a little more to be persuasive.

To select the right button, you might think of debtors as falling into one of five different categories, each one responding most strongly to one of the five basic needs. Information about income, lifestyle, and type of debt can be used in deciding how to categorize the debtor most appropriately. These groups are listed below.

Group One. These are people who are concerned about survival or about losing the security they have. These people are especially concerned about taking care of monthly bills. Frequently they have low or below-average incomes, and their main concern is making it. They often have trouble paying debts because they have difficulty getting by and managing money. A key way to appeal to people like this is to reassure them that paying the debt will give them less to worry about. They won't have to worry about losing essential property or services, as they might if the matter ends up in court; and they will avoid hassles with the big institutions they often fear, like the banks, police, and courts.

Group Two. These are people who want comfort and ease and are especially concerned about losing the income or property that gives them a comfortable lifestyle. These people want to do more than just "make it" and pay the bills. They want a comfortable life in which they can take it easy and relax. They might be especially interested in a nice home in the suburbs, a car, and the usual conveniences, or they might be satisfied with a modest apartment or condominium in the city. Frequently, these are blue collar and office workers with middle-level jobs who see themselves as part of the mainstream and feel they need the appropriate material items and income to keep up. Obviously, an appeal to the maintenance of comfort, or to the possibility of losing that comfort, is one approach to consider in collecting from this group.

Group Three. These are people who seek belonging, love, and affection, and are especially concerned about anything that affects their ability to gain this. These people are very interested in being with others and feeling acceptance and social approval. They want to be thought of as good, honest, trustworthy people. Those with a more settled, middle-income lifestyle are often eager to fit into their community and be accepted, while others, especially the young and single, may crave travel, adventure, and fun, interesting friends. They see money as a way to satisfy their need to fit in or have fun and meet interesting people, and often they take on debts they can't afford while trying to keep pace with others in the community or in their social set. You can point out, in trying to collect from such people, that keeping up with others and maintaining a good reputation will be impossible if major debts are ignored for too long.

Group Four. These are people who seek recognition, and fear anything that damages their self-esteem, pride, or reputation. Such people typically want power, prestige, or respect from others. They are especially interested in proving their self-worth through their achievement or trappings of success. You'll typically find such people among those on the way up, trying hard to make it in some field, or among those who have already attained a position of power in business, politics, or the arts. Often they end up spending too much by trying to impress others. The appeal that particularly motivates them is any threat to their power, prestige, or self-respect.

Group Five. These are people who seek self-fulfillment and are especially concerned about anything that limits their freedom for creative expression or accomplishing personal goals. These people are a little out of the ordinary and can be found in all walks of life, though they are less likely to be among those who are just making it. These people are essentially very inner directed, and want to achieve goals or ideals they have set for themselves. They often end up in debt because they have a vision they are not able to achieve, and they may remain in debt because they hope to achieve that vision. With them, a key appeal is to their desire to achieve and continue to be creative.

To some extent, all of us share the characteristics just listed, and may respond to any number of appeals. The advantage of categorizing the debtor, however, is that some people respond more to certain appeals than to others. If you can assess the debtor appropriately, you can emphasize the corresponding appeal and be more effective in selling the debtor on paying you.

If you have limited information, however, rely on the broad general appeals that are widely applicable to everyone, such as having a good reputation, being an honorable, responsible person, maintaining comfort and security, and being liked.

Examples of Statements that Back Up Your Appeals

Following are some examples of statements that express the five major appeals. Use them to give you ideas on what to say when you write or speak to the debtor.

Appeals to the Need for Self-Preservation and Safety

"You won't have to worry about this unpaid bill anymore."

"You'll feel more secure after you've taken care of your debts."

"You might not get the credit you need in the future if you don't pay this bill."

"If you don't pay your bills, you could endanger your credit and face other problems. For example, some employers look at their employees' credit ratings, and this can affect your future promotion."

"You wouldn't want your employer to think you didn't pay your bills, would you? They would find out if we have to go to court and garnish your wages. That could cause you a lot of problems in the future."

"If we don't get your payment today, we'll have to take further action which could result in an inconvenience for you in the future."

"You'll save money by paying this now. If not, we'll have to add interest and other charges."

"It will be much more expensive for you in the long run if you do not pay."

Appeals to the Need for Comfort and Ease

"You'll feel relieved when this is over, and you won't have to worry about us contacting you again."

"We'd like to be able to continue to extend you credit so you can continue to take advantage of our special sales and layaway purchase plan, which is designed to make everything easy for you, as one of our valued customers."

"You have a lovely home, and when you need new furniture, you'll probably want to use your credit again. So I'm sure you want to keep your good credit rating."

"You don't want to lose your attractive living room set, do you?"

Appeals to the Need for Belonging, Love and Affection

"You value our friendship, don't you? Then I hope you won't let this debt stand in the way of our continued friendship, and that you'll pay me back as you promised."

"Your family will appreciate you for taking care of this matter now. You wouldn't want to put them in a situation where you can't get credit when you need it, would you?"

"You want the other members of your family to respect you, don't you? When you pay your bills, you set a good example for your children."

"You've got a good name in your community as a responsible person who pays her bills on time. We hope you want to keep your reputation that way."

Appeals to the Need for Self-Esteem

"You are a responsible, trustworthy person, aren't you? Then, pay this bill as you agreed."

"You want to think of yourself as an honest and reliable person, don't you?"

"I know you face your obligations and responsibilities. Well, this is your responsibility and you should take care of it."

"I'm sure you can understand the difficulties your non-payment has caused our company. We appeal to your sense of responsibility and concern for others. Please pay us the money that is due."

"I'm sure if you look to your own conscience, it'll tell you that it's only right to pay the bill and it's wrong not to pay."

"You made a promise to pay this when you borrowed money from me. So come on; live up to the promise you made."

"We extended credit to you in good faith and have been fair to you. You want to be fair with us and show good faith, too, don't you?"

"You already have a good payment record with us. We hope you'll want to keep your good credit record."

"You want to keep your good reputation in the community, don't you?" (Don't threaten to do anything to tarnish it yourself.)

Appeals to the Need for Self-Fulfillment

"You can't gain true success in the long run if you don't live up to your personal obligations."

"I'm all for your efforts to become successful, and I'd like to help you achieve this. But if I'm going to continue to support you, I need you to show your good faith and pay me the money you promised."

"We'd like to continue to help you meet your personal goals with our program. But we can't unless you pay us the balance due."

"I have an idea that will help you achieve your goal and also pay me back the money you owe me. Let's sit down and talk about it."

CHAPTER 13:
Effective Use
of the Appeals

Once you have a sense of who the debtor is or what appeals might work best, start with one appeal or a combination of appeals. Then, if you need follow-up letters, calls, or meetings, use variations on this same theme or try another appeal.

If there is a possibility that a dispute may be the reason for nonpayment (such as a controversy over the amount due), or if the debtor may be having difficulty paying, leave a door open for discussion or negotiation. For example, combine your appeals with a statement that you assume the debtor accepts the validity of the debt; however, if there is any question, or if the debtor is having some trouble paying, he or she should let you know at once so you can discuss this.

The advantage of such an approach is that debtors often ignore statements if they don't think they owe the money or can't pay, but will respond if you specifically let them know you are open to discussion. Furthermore, when you state that you assume the debt is valid unless they contest it, you are in a stronger position to argue that they owe the debt if you go to court.

There's no absolute science to the appeals process. But after a while you'll get a feeling for what works with different debtors.

Finally, a word of advice. Though fear can be a very effective motivator, save the heavy appeals to the end of the appeals process or, better yet, wait until your final demand. You want to maintain the debtor's good will until the end. Guarded hints, such as saying you would be sorry if you lost your good relationship over this matter, are fine. But stay away from heavy threats about possibly serious losses until later. You also want to avoid stepping over the fine line between appealing to the debtor's self-interest and making threats that seem like undue pressure and extortion.

The following section describes each of the major appeals in more detail and includes some sample letters and conversations with the debtor using each appeal. Adapt these to your own style. We'll start with the higher order appeals first.

Appeals to the Need for Self-Fulfillment

These appeals to self-fulfillment include the appeal to the debtor's: desire for success; desire to achieve personal goals and engage in creative expression; sympathy and concern for the well-being of others; and feelings of guilt for unethical behavior.

While there may be some overlap with the need for belonging or prestige, in that acquiring these qualities can help the individual win friends, gain esteem, and do better financially, the focus is on the person's inner sense of self. It's a good appeal for people who like to think of themselves as moral, ethical, well-intentioned, sincere, honest, and/or religious.

The Desire for Success

This appeal is based on suggesting that you can help the debtor gain greater success if he or she pays the bill. It's an approach that works particularly well with the upwardly mobile. If such debtors have limited funds, and you convince them you can help them more than other creditors, they are likely to pay you first.

(In a letter:)
Dear Mr. Smith:

When a person like yourself appreciates the finer things of life, we like to do everything we can to help.

So far we have been at your service by supplying you with the finest in quality products. But now your account of $600 is over two months overdue.

We certainly want to go on helping you as we have in the past. So please, send in your payment in the next few days, so we can continue to contribute to making your life a pleasure and a success.

Sincerely,

(In a phone call:)
Hi Joe . . .

I've got some great news to let you know about . . . and also a little matter to clear up.

But first the good news. I've got special tickets to a business networking party, and there will be a chance to make a special presentation for new business.

Also, on the other matter, I still haven't gotten the check you promised to send. I'd like to get it settled, so we don't have this standing in the way of our working together on all the great things we have planned.

The Desire to Achieve Personal Goals and Engage in Creative Expression

The strategy here is to show the debtor how you can help him or her gain a desired goal, if the outstanding debt is attended to. By seeing you as a valuable contributor, the debtor will want to make sure you get paid.

In the long run, you may not want to engage in further business dealings with a person who is essentially a manipulator, who will only pay obligations if there seems to be a pay-off. But if you've gotten into a situation with someone like this, this suggestion that you can help is one way of getting paid. Once that happens, you can always end the relationship.

> (In a letter:)
> Dear Terry:
> Since you are always looking for ways to travel and reduce costs, I thought I'd send along the following packet of information on setting up special tours with people you know. You can make money as well as get free travel. I can help you set up the program, if you're interested.
> Also, I still haven't gotten payment of $250 for the books you sold for me. I'd like to get this resolved in the next few days and I'll look forward to getting your payment.
> Sincerely,

> (In a phone call:)
> Hi Tony...I just met some people in the travel business who would like to collaborate with a trade show promoter and market trips to people who attend the show. We've been working out an arrangement where we can make money for you. You won't have to do anything but give us space. I'd like to set up a meeting to talk about it.
> Incidentally, I'm still waiting for that commission check of $500 you promised. If you can bring the check along to our meeting, that'll be great.

Guilt or Sympathy and Concern for the Well-Being of Others

This appeal emphasizes that the creditor has done the debtor a favor; it is designed to make the debtor feel sympathetic or guilty that he or she has inconvenienced or caused the creditor to suffer by not paying the debt. With some debtors the guilt appeal is especially effective.

However, this appeal only works if there is a real basis for feeling sympathy for you as a creditor. If you are well-off and you try to sound like you're suffering while the debtor is struggling to survive, your appeal will sound ludicrous. It only works when the debtor can afford to pay and his or her failure to pay has caused you financial problems.

Before you use this appeal, also be sure the debtor is the type of person who is likely to feel guilty or sympathetic. There's no point in using this approach with someone who probably won't care.

Be certain you sound believable, and don't go too far in making extravagant claims to provoke sympathy or guilt. You don't want it to seem as if you are groveling for the money, or list so many problems that you sound like a social welfare case with an absurd claim.

Pitch your appeal to the kind of person who might be sympathetic, and be sensible in making your appeal.

> (In a letter:)
> Dear Walt:
>
> The $500 you still owe for the books you bought from me is creating some serious problems for our company.
>
> As you know, we're a small struggling company, and we gave you these books on credit with the understanding that you would pay us in the next few days.
>
> Now it's been over two months and we still haven't got the money. We put up several hundred dollars ourselves to pay for these books and we really can't afford to carry your account like this.
>
> So, please, please, send us your check today. We'd like to be able to continue doing business together, and we need your cooperation to do so.

> (In a phone call.)
> Hello, Joe . . . This is _____. Please, I've got to get that payment you promised by Friday, or I'm going to have some problems.
>
> I've been stalling the landlord about the rent, but she's about ready to give up on me, and if I keep paying late, it will be impossible for me to negotiate the lease when it expires at the end of the year. Also, I've got to take the company van in for some engine work.
>
> So can I count on you to get me that payment?

Appeals to the Need for Self-Esteem

The appeals related to the debtor's need for self-esteem include appeals to the debtor's: sense of integrity, honesty, fairness, and justice; pride and self-respect; and to the desire to maintain a good reputation with others.

These appeals are directed to the debtor who is concerned with maintaining a good, successful image of him or herself or his or her company. While a desire for self-fulfillment, especially success, may contribute to the debtor's feelings of esteem, these appeals stress the image or appearance the debtor presents and his or her concern with what others think.

The Sense of Personal Integrity, Honesty, Fairness, and Justice

This appeal is designed to make the debtor feel he or she is not being honest or fair in dealing with the creditor, and that it is only just to pay the money owed. The main idea to get across is that it's unfair not to pay or to delay payment to the creditor.

This appeal works particularly well with people who want to see themselves as solid, respectable citizens; with firms that pride themselves on their good reputations; and with friends and close business associates with whom you have had a good relationship.

In making this appeal, you should emphasize why the debtor is not being fair. Point out that you have done everything the debtor asked, and mention other ways you have been helpful to the debtor. For example, stress how you did a favor, provided a valuable service or product, or were especially prompt in getting the debtor a desired item.

In a sense, you are acting like the debtor's conscience by pointing out how he or she has wronged you. Yet, you don't want to sound too heavy in this moral guardian role, or you can provoke resentment. Just be tactful and respectful in telling the debtor that he or she has been unfair.

> (In a letter:)
> Dear Jack:
> I'm surprised you didn't send the $300 due in response to my reminder last month. As you know, when I came to speak to your group I went out of my way to change my schedule to accommodate you, and I did you a favor by printing up some flyers. You got an especially big turn-out, and the response to the speech was extremely good. I feel I certainly kept my commitment, and I hope I can count on you to be fair and keep our agreement, too.
> Sincerely,

(In a phone call:)

Hello. . . This is _____ calling about the check. I thought you were going to leave a check for $250 for me at your office, but when I stopped by it wasn't there. You asked me to write up that material for you, and I got it written and copied for you overnight. You also said you would reimburse me my out-of-pocket costs in doing the project, but you haven't.

Don't you think it's only fair you take care of this now? After all, that was our agreement, and I've done everything you asked.

Pride and Self-Respect

The underlying message of this appeal is that the debtor should want to do the right and honorable thing in paying an honest debt. Conversely, he or she should feel that it is shameful and embarrassing to be in debt. In some cases a creditor can proceed on the assumption the debtor wants to continue to look good to the creditor, because they have had past business dealings or have been friends. Overall, this is a good appeal to use with an individual or company that wants to maintain a valued reputation or image of success.

(In a letter:)

Dear Ms. Allen:

It's hard to understand why you haven't paid your out-standing bill of $300.

You've always been a good customer in the past, and we have regarded you highly because you've always been so prompt in paying your bills.

But now your account is nearly two months past due. Won't you send us your check, so we can continue to give you our highest rating as a valued customer?

(In a phone call:)

Hi Joe . . . I'm calling about your printing bill for $500, which is still due. You've always been one of our best accounts, and so we're surprised this bill is still outstanding. Perhaps it's been an oversight, or you've been busy, but we'd like to be able to continue our top rating for you. So--can I count on you to get a check in the mail to us today?

The Desire to Maintain a Good Reputation with Others

This appeal is similar to the appeal to the debtor's pride and self-respect except that it focuses on the people in the community the debtor wants to impress, not just you. When you use this appeal, you can imply that since the debtor wants to look good to others, he or she might have problems if people knew that legitimate debts tend to go unpaid. But be careful to avoid directly threatening to defame the debtor's character; defaming a person is illegal, and the threat borders on extortion, which is also illegal.

(In a letter:)

Dear Mr. Franklin:

Certainly your firm prides itself on its reputation in the community. So that's why it surprises us that your account for $500 has still not been paid, though we have written to you about this several times in the last three months.

Since your firm is on the board of several community groups, we felt sure we wouldn't have any problems with getting paid. So please, get your check in the mail today.

We hope you will continue to live up to your excellent past reputation for responsibility and excellence.

Sincerely,

(In a phone call:)

Hi, Joe . . . First, I wanted to offer my compliments, since I just heard about the great things you've been doing at your office recently. I can see you really understand the value of good public relations.

Secondly, I wanted to let you know your bill for $250 for the office supplies is still unpaid. I know you've been involved in building up your contacts in the community lately, so perhaps you've been busy.

But that's all the more reason to take care of these things. After all, I'm sure you value your reputation with us, don't you?

Can you get your check off to us today, so we can settle this matter?

Appeals to the Need for Belonging

This appeal is directed to the debtor's concern with being liked and fitting into the community or to a special interest peer group, such as the "yuppie" business-professional community. While the desire to belong can involve a concern with maintaining a good reputation, the emphasis in this appeal is on the feeling of belonging rather than on gaining the honor, prestige, and reputation that helps one belong.

The major appeals in this category include the appeal to the debtor's: desire to be a respected, accepted member of the community; desire to keep pace with the crowd, have fun, and meet interesting people; and his or her desire to gain love, affection, and romance.

The flip side, of course, is that the debtor will lose these desired benefits if he or she doesn't pay.

The Desire to be a Respected, Accepted Member of the Community

This approach emphasizes that respectable, responsible members of the community pay their bills on time; therefore, if the debtor wants to be an accepted part of this community, he or she should pay, too. It's an approach that works well with settled residents, particularly in smaller or suburban communities.

(In a letter:)
Dear Mrs. Jones:

Your charge account for $250 has been overdue for three months, and you have ignored our friendly reminders.

You've been given charge privileges at our store because you were recommended to us as a responsible member of your community who pays her bills on time. And we're certain you will want to keep your good rating.

So please, don't risk your excellent credit record over this. You need a good rating for so many things you want to do.

Now won't you get your payment to us in the mail today?
Sincerely,

(In a phone call:)

Hi Mary . . . I'm calling for the Business and Professional Club because we haven't gotten your check for $100 membership, though we got your renewal and sent you several reminders.

Now, as an active member of the community, surely you want to keep your accounts up to date and not miss out on the chance to be included in our directory.

So, please, can you send in your check today, and we'll reinstate your membership in good standing at once.

The Desire to Keep Pace with the Crowd and Have Fun

The main emphasis here is on what the debtor will be missing if he or she doesn't pay. This approach is especially appropriate for a social club where a person has signed a membership contract or has requested a renewal but hasn't paid.

(In a letter:)
Dear Mrs. Williams:

All kinds of exciting activities will be coming up in the next three months; surely you don't want to miss them.

A barbecue on a glorious country estate in July . . . a cruise on an elegant steamboat in August . . . a gala party in the most fabulous mansion in September. See our enclosed flyer for details.

Unfortunately, we haven't received the balance of $250 due on your membership and we can't include you on the invitation list until your payment arrives. Won't you send in your check today, so you won't miss out?

Sincerely,

(In a phone call:)

Hi Nancy . . . I thought you wanted to come to the gala ski weekend I'm planning. We've got the cabin and are setting up some special tours for our group now.

However, before I can go ahead and include you, we've got to take care of that little personal matter between us. You said you were going to be sending me $50, but I never received it. So, can you get that in the mail tonight?   Then I'll go ahead and hold a place for you.

The Desire to Gain Love and Affection

Probably the most likely time to use this approach is when you have a personal friendship with someone who hasn't paid. In this case the suggestion is that the person may lose your friendship if he or she doesn't pay.

When you make such an appeal to a person you are close to, you are taking the risk that you may lose their affection and friendship. However, if the person has been avoiding a debt for some time, you are carrying someone around who isn't pulling his or her fair weight and you may not want to keep a relationship going anyway.

To maintain good will if you can, be firm but diplomatic when you make this appeal.

(In a letter:)
Dear Joe:

It bothers me very much to write this letter, since I have always considered you a close friend.

But I feel I trusted you in a matter a few months ago, and now I'm not sure if I may not have made a mistake.

I extended your business a $1000 credit line when you were in a tight spot. You assured me that you would pay us monthly.

Since then, you have been telling me one reason or another why you can't pay. I feel we made a firm commitment when I set up your credit line, and I did so because you needed it very much and you were my friend.

However, now it's been over three months, and you haven't paid us anything. I really need this money now myself to pay some of my own unexpected bills this month, and I would like to get it back in the next few days.

I sure would hate to have our long friendship disturbed over this matter.

Sincerely,

(In a phone call.)

Hi there, Eddy . . . I thought you were my friend, and we could trust each other. Well, I still haven't gotten paid that $230 for the landscaping work I performed for you. I know it's not a very large amount, but we had an agreement, and you've been telling me for some time that you were going to pay me. So how about it? Let's get this whole thing up to date, and then we don't have to worry about some stupid debt coming up and disturbing our friendship. Well, what do you say?

Appeals to the Need for Comfort and Ease

With this appeal, you're zeroing in on the debtor's property and possessions and the things that make living or doing business relatively easy and comfortable. The positive side of this appeal is offering the debtor additional opportunities to acquire the things he or she wants to make life or business function more easily. The negative side is threatening the reduce the debtor's ease and comfort by taking away the things he or she has that promote this satisfying way of life.

In particular, the appeals related to the debtor's need for comfort and ease include: a desire for a comfortable lifestyle with a nice home, car, or conveniences; and a desire for things to run smoothly and to avoid everyday problems and hassles.

While this appeal can be used for debtors in a broad range of incomes, it's particularly effective with the middle income and working class debtor, who has the traditional values of living a comfortable life.

The Desire for a Comfortable Lifestyle with a Nice Home, Car, or Conveniences

The emphasis in this appeal is on living the good comfortable life. You can stress either the comforts that result or the material items that give the debtor this comfortable lifestyle.

When you first appeal to the debtor, stress the positive aspects of this appeal. If he or she pays the bill, you'll extend more credit, so more purchases can be made. As the debtor delays and delays, switch to the negative side of this appeal and talk about taking things away.

(In a letter, stressing the positive:)
Dear Ms. Allen:

Your credit account with our store is seriously overdue-- and it's very close to our limit of $1,000.

We know you as a customer who appreciates the finer things in life, and that's why we've continued to extend you credit. We'd like to be able to keep doing this so you can take advantage of the special offers on new clothing and jewelry that we make to our regular charge account customers.

But first we have to get your account current. So please send in your regular $100 monthly payment today, and as soon as we receive it, we'll send you our list of specials for January.

Sincerely,

(In a letter, stressing the negative:)
Dear Ms. Thomas:

The bill for the couch you bought from our store three months ago is still unpaid. The balance remaining is $400.

We're surprised you ignored our several reminders, since our contract states we can take back the couch if you don't pay us each month until the balance is paid.

You may find it uncomfortable to find yourself without a couch in your living room, and we would prefer not to have to take any action in this matter.

So, please send us your monthly payment and keep your couch.

Sincerely,

The same message can be conveyed by phone.

The Desire to Avoid Everyday Hassles

In this appeal you point out to the debtor that, since the bill will have to be paid eventually, the best option is to avoid the everyday hassle that will occur from not paying it (such as more letters, phone calls, and invoices). You can also point out that once the matter is closed, the debtor will experience a sense of relief and peace of mind.

When you make this appeal, don't sound threatening, as if you plan to harass the debtor, which is illegal. Instead, simply observe that many debtors experience their debts as a burden and are relieved to get rid of them.

> (In a letter:)
> Dear Mr. Henry:
> You are probably tired of getting still another bill from us, and frankly, we'd like it if we didn't have to keep sending them.
> You probably don't like our reminder calls either, and we'd rather not make them, either.
> So why don't you send us the balance of $225 as you promised, and we can close out this matter once and for all.
> You'll be relieved to have this off your mind--and certainly, we will, too.
> Sincerely,

> (In a phone call:)
> Hi Fred . . . What happened?   I thought you were sending me that check. I hate to keep calling you about this, and I'm sure you're getting pretty sick of my reminders. So what do you say? Let's get this thing taken care of once and for all, and then you don't have to worry about me bugging you anymore. And I can think of lots of other things I'd rather talk about with you anytime.

Appeals to the Need for Safety and Security

This is a last-resort type of appeal, since you are using fear as a motivator and your tone is somewhat more insistent and threatening. As a rule, you should reserve this for your last step before moving on to your final demand.

To be effective and protect yourself legally, keep your warning somewhat veiled. Make an implied threat, not an overt one. Suggest it's in the debtor's best interest to pay the amount due immediately; otherwise, something unfortunate may happen (for example, the individual or business may lose the ability to gain credit or the person's job or business may be at risk). However, don't come right out and say you are going to see that any of these things occur, because that can be interpreted as extortion. In addition, the debtor may feel so resentful that he or she will feel justified in refusing to pay.

Major appeals in this category include: the ability to survive or feel secure as an individual; and the ability to survive or prosper as a business.

The Ability to Survive or Feel Secure as an Individual

The survival-security appeal works particularly well with the low-income individual who owes money, since he or she is already dealing with such issues on an everyday basis. This person commonly gets into debt because he or she has trouble getting by and may try to avoid debts that aren't immediately pressing. To get paid you may have to make the person concerned that nonpayment may interfere with his or her ability to make it. Then, too, many of these people are a little frightened or awed by the big established institutions that help creditors collect (like courts and collection agencies). References to these can sometimes help your case.

> (In a letter:)
> Dear Mr. Andrews:
>
> You have already ignored several of our requests for payment of $125 on the couch you have bought.
>
> We have tried to be patient, but we feel we will have to act soon to show that we are serious.
>
> As you may know, your contract makes you liable for payments, and when these aren't received, we have the right to pursue a number of legal channels to obtain our payment. For example, after a court decision against you, part of your wages could be used to pay us; there are other alternatives as well.
>
> However, you can avoid all these problems by simply sending us a check or money order for the amount due.
>
> Sincerely,

(In a phone call:)

Hello, Mrs. Evans . . . This is _____. We still haven't gotten your payment of $125, and it's been about 3 weeks. I'm sure you're getting tired of our frequent reminders, and we sure don't want to have to end up in court with you or possibly have to take the money out of your wages. So, can I count on you this time to get it in?

The Ability to Survive or Prosper as a Business

This approach to businesses is particularly appropriate with a company that has a pattern of poor payment, either because the owner is negligent or because the company has been having financial problems for some time. An owner in these circumstances is probably not going to be responsive to appeals for fairness, justice, or maintaining a good reputation because his or her main concern is whether the business will survive.

Direct your appeal accordingly. If you are an important supplier, you might threaten to cut off future business if the company can't pay. Or you might persuade the owner to settle up if he or she thinks your legal efforts to collect can threaten the company's ability to survive.

You may lose the company as a future business associate with this type of appeal. But then, if you have to make this appeal to get paid, you probably don't care that much about keeping the company's business. Or if you do continue to do business, it probably should be on a cash-on-delivery basis.

(In a letter:)
Dear Ms. Williams:

We're disappointed that you still haven't sent in your payment for your unpaid balance of $200. When you asked us to ship on credit, we agreed because we trusted you, but you have not done as you promised.

Surely you realize that you need to maintain a good credit standing and the good will of your important suppliers. Otherwise, people in the trade will hear about this, and you will have problems getting needed supplies.

Still, we are hopeful you may regain our trust by sending in the balance due promptly. So please mail your check to us today.

Let's resolve this situation now, so we can go on from here in a new spirit of mutual benefit and trust.

Sincerely,

(In a phone call.)

Hi Larry . . . We still haven't gotten your check for $200. You know, we've been trusting you, and we still hope we can. But unless we get this payment in the next few days, we're going to have to cross you off the list of people we work with. And I know that will make it difficult for your business, since you'll have to go out of town to buy. Besides, you know what a tight little business community this is here. So come on. Can we count on your check by Friday, so we can consider this situation resolved?

Combining Your Appeals

Combining several appeals in the same letter can be effective, because you are motivating the debtor to pay on several levels simultaneously. Select the strongest appeals for a particular debtor and use these.

For example, the following letter combines appeals to self-interest, fairness, and justice.

Dear Mr. Jackson:

Why have you ignored our many invoices for your balance of $675? In doing so, you are not being fair, since we bent over backwards in getting the materials you wanted to you faster than usual.

Your failure to respond is forcing us to consider other action, and we hate to do this, because we both lose. We lose you as a customer, and you lose us as a supplier, after a long and mutually beneficial relationship.

Please don't put us in a position where we must take other action to collect. This is what we will have to do if we don't receive your full payment by Friday the 15th.

Please, mail in your check today, and let's continue our previously good relationship.

Sincerely,

The following letter mixes together pride, self-interest, and the prospect of losing a comfortable arrangement.

Dear Mr. Davis:

You have been enjoying the pride of owning one of the finest stereo sets on the market since June. The styling is designed for maximum comfort in listening.

However, your last three payments are past due, for a total of $700. Surely you'd like to continue to enjoy the pleasure of these items. Especially when you were lucky enough to buy them on sale and save 35% off the regular cost.

If we don't receive your payment, we'll have to take these items back.

I'm sure you'll agree it isn't worth it to risk losing the advantage of this wonderful system. So please send your check today, or call me so we can work out a solution.

Sincerely,

Combining Your Appeals with an Opportunity for Discussion or Negotiation

You'll notice the last letter had the tag line, "or call me so we can work out a solution." Such an offer to discuss the matter is an excellent way to create an opening, so the debtor can discuss why he or she hasn't paid or try to work out a settlement.

Some creditors suggest having a discussion in the reminder phase. However, it's usually best at that point to assume the debtor owes the debt, unless he or she voluntarily questions it or refers to payment problems.

Later, though, when you start making appeals or have made a few of them, it's appropriate to raise the matter yourself. Since the debtor hasn't paid you after a number of requests, you want to know why.

When you suggest having a discussion or working out a settlement, you can do so in several ways. You can ask the debtor to write you explaining the problem. You can suggest the debtor call you to discuss the matter or work out a solution. Or you can offer to sit down and discuss the matter. If it's a small amount or if the debtor is an individual customer, suggest a visit to your place; conversely, if the amount is quite large and the debtor has a business, it might be better to meet at the debtor's office, so you can check out the viability of the business.

CHAPTER 14:
Adapting Your
Appeals to
the Debtor

The appeals process described in the previous chapter is a typical approach used by professional collectors in dealing with most debtors. You seek payment in full, and you use increasingly intense appeals to motivate the debtor.

However, at times you need to vary your approach to deal with certain circumstances. For example, if you think the debtor may be having problems paying in full, you can suggest that you are open to an alternate payment arrangement. Another possibility in some situations is to develop a creative payment program where the debtor pays you in merchandise or services, or pays you by continuing to buy needed products or services from you, but adds a little bit extra to pay off the past debt. Then, too, if the debtor has failed to follow through in paying you through the usual channels (such as sending a check by mail), you may need to show you are willing to take extra steps to make it easier for the debtor to pay.

The following chapter describes these methods of adapting the appeals process. Be creative; devise other strategies to suit your situation.

Suggesting Alternatives if the
Debtor Can't Pay in Full

Although it's preferable to request immediate payment in full in your first appeal and leave it up to the debtor to request other terms, there are times when a debtor may be too embarrassed to admit to financial problems.

If you suspect this might be the case, you might suggest you are open to an alternate payment arrangement if the person has problems paying. If you think the debtor might have some question or complaint about the debt, you might mention this too. For example, your last appeals letter or call might include a statement like this:

Since you haven't responded to any of our reminders or previous appeals, is there some problem we can discuss? We'd like to work it out with you if there is. If you have any difficulty paying the requested amount in full, we might be able to work out a special arrangement with you. And if you have any question or complaint about the bill, now is the time to let us know.

If the debtor responds with a grievance, there are methods for handling this; these are discussed in a later section of this book. Assuming for now that the problem is the person's ability to pay the bill, there are four major arrangements you can suggest: extending the account through a deferred payment; accepting a postdated check; accepting a series of partial payments; or writing up a promissory note held by a third party.

Extending the Account Through a Deferred Payment

In effect, you are suggesting the debtor continue doing what he or she is already doing--extending the date when the account is supposed to be paid. However, by formally extending the account, you are taking pressure off the debtor and thereby promoting good will. A common arrangement is for 30 days. But make this suggestion only if you feel the debtor can and will pay at this time. Otherwise you are simply giving the debtor a free ride for the extension period; at the end he or she may simply ignore your debt. When you enter into this agreement, ask for some formal assurance that the debtor will pay you by a given date (such as a signed letter of agreement). Also be sure the debtor has a good explanation of why he or she missed the original payment date.

Accepting a Postdated Check

This approach is like extending the account, only you have the promised payment in hand (assuming the check is good). If the check bounces, at least you are in a stronger legal position to collect.

Accepting such a check makes the most sense in a situation where the debtor currently doesn't have the money, but is expecting some money soon. Make sure the debtor really is likely to get this money and is not just giving you some hopeful story. Bear in mind that some debtors pass dozens of bad checks this way, appealing constantly to expected bank loans that never materialize or other "ships about to come in." Too often, trusting creditors end up with nothing more than promises and worthless checks. Don't let that happen to you.

Accepting a Series of Partial Payments

In this fairly common arrangement you suggest the debtor make a series of payments, working out an amount the debtor can pay. For example, you might divide up the total into four to six payments to be paid over a like period of months, with the first payment to be made immediately. Then the debtor makes another payment each month.

In some cases, creditors choose not to charge interest in order to show good will. But it's fair to add on a reasonable interest charge if you want to propose this.

Writing Up a Promissory Note Payable By the Bank

If the amount due is substantial, you might ask the debtor to give you a promissory note to pay you for the full amount of the debt, plus interest for the amount of time over which he or she will pay off the note. In this case the key difference from other notes that are just promises (and sometimes quite empty ones), is that this note is not made out to you, but to a third party, usually a bank, to whom the debtor makes the payment. The third party pays you. In effect, the debtor is taking out a loan to pay you in full. The promissory note is his or her agreement to pay off the lender.

Getting Paid on the Continued Business Plan

If the debtor hasn't been able to pay, and you have a product or service he or she still wants, you can promote continued business and get paid at the same time. Offer to continue doing business with the debtor on a "C.O.D. plus" basis. According to this arrangement, the debtor can still buy your products or services, but pays C.O.D. plus a little extra to retire the old debt.

The best time to use this strategy is when you see that the debtor is struggling, and that he or she needs what you offer to stay in business-- and could possibly get it from a competitor. Such a person might continue to be a good paying customer if you continue to do business together until better times come along.

Tell the debtor you can't extend any more credit, but will be glad to provide what is needed, at the usual rates, if payment is up front and an effort is made to work off the debt. The result is a win-win situation. The debtor gets what he or she needs for business, and you gradually get your money while maintaining the debtor's business and good will.

Taking Extra Steps to Get Your Money

In making your appeal, you normally want the debtor to pay you through the usual channels, such as mailing you the money or stopping by with a check. As a rule, you shouldn't offer to make a special trip to the debtor's business or home; you could end up spending a lot of time and gas money driving around to collect debts. Professional collectors call this "setting up a bread run." You should avoid it if you can.

However, if the sum is substantial, and if you are beginning to doubt the debtor's promises and feel a personal appearance by you or your messenger will give you the extra push you need, take the extra step of making in-person contact. My friend Andy, who ran a $200 ad for a local promoter, got numerous excuses and no payment--as did dozens of the business' other creditors. He decided to make a personal appearance to press for payment. Andy drove directly to the promoter's office, walked past the secretary, and demanded a check. "You've been giving me excuses for the last three weeks," he said. "Since you're a going business, you must have at least $200 available in your account. This has been going on long enough. Pay up." And the promoter did--to avoid an argument in front of his staff with a man who looked like he wouldn't leave without a call to the police.

Of course, such a confrontational approach runs the risk of being considered harassment, defamation, or extortion, and carries the kinds of potential problems discussed earlier in this book. If you come on too strong, you may get into trouble; yet often, as in the case I've just described, a one-on-one strategy works when applied judiciously.

Even if you don't feel comfortable playing the tough-guy role, you can still convey firmness with your personal appearance and give your appeal extra clout. For example, offer to wait to resolve the matter until you get to see the debtor. Suggest that you will be going directly from your visit to the courthouse if you cannot sit down and talk about the matter now. Or make a remark using one of the appeals already described, such as, "I know you value your reputation and want to be fair in paying your debts. So let's discuss this and get the matter resolved."

CHAPTER 15:
Discussing the Bill With the Debtor

After you've made several appeals to the debtor, but have still not received payment, you know you have a problem. Sometimes the debtor will tell you directly; often he or she will simply ignore any written requests or phone messages. Some debtors will agree to pay when you speak to each other, simply to get you to go away, and then won't pay.

You have a choice: deal directly with the debtor to discuss the matter, or give up and move on to the final push. Since it's to your advantage to settle without getting tough and involving a lawyer, collection agency, or the courts, now's the time to get some dialogue going and find out the real cause for the debtor's not paying the bill. Only by dealing with that cause are you likely to get the debtor to pay.

The Five Major Reasons for Non-Payment

Once you find out the real reason the debtor isn't paying, you can work on resolving the situation by finding a more compelling appeal to motivate payment. You need to do this to get your money because you have to make the debtor's motive to pay more compelling than his or her resistance to paying. In order to change this balance in your favor, you must understand why the debtor has been resisting. Then you can more effectively appeal to his or her needs and overcome resistance. In short, you have to be both a problem-solver and a salesperson. If you are effective, you'll get your money.

There are five main reasons for non-payment.

(1) The debtor can't (or believes he or she can't) pay the whole amount, but is open to working out payment agreements.

(2) The debtor wants to stall, because he or she is uncertain as to whether to acknowledge responsibility for the debt. Or, if the debtor accepts the debt, he or she isn't ready to pay.

(3) The debtor has a real grievance or dispute, and doesn't believe he or she should owe either all or part of the debt.

(4) The debtor is intentionally trying to avoid paying the debt by avoiding the creditor or making up excuses. (Sometimes this debtor is called a "credit criminal.")

(5) The debtor has become handicapped or destitute and truly can't pay anything now, although he or she may be able to pay later.

When you understand the debtor, you can respond accordingly; realize, however, that a given debtor can shift from one category to another depending on circumstances and on your own responses. For example, if you come down too hard on a debtor who acknowledges the debt, can't pay in full, and is open to payment arrangements, you can alienate the debtor. The debtor may decide he or she has a real grievance, and that it's appropriate not to pay. Likewise, if you wait too long to ask for payment from a debtor who is having trouble paying, he or she may turn into a real hardship case with no money.

Once you assess the situation, act fairly and quickly to get the money that's due as soon as you can.

Finding Out About the Debtor

To determine the real reason for nonpayment and find out how to motivate the debtor or reduce resistance, you have to learn to listen and develop a rapport with the debtor. When you speak, say what you mean; avoid being misunderstood.

Keep your message simple and brief, so the debtor easily understands what you are trying to say. Avoid trying to impress with long words. You will only confuse or alienate the debtor.

For example, when you state the problem, say something like, "You promised to pay us for the furniture when you bought it, and now you have to pay the bill," or, "I made a loan to you in good faith, and I'd like to get my money back now." Stay away from statements like, "I'm sure you understood that the contract you signed when you purchased the merchandise committed you to a definite obligation to make regular payments. Now you are required to make payment in keeping with the agreement you signed."

Establish rapport with the debtor from the first moment you start to talk about the debt. If you don't know the debtor, be courteous and polite, yet firm and businesslike. You want to treat the debtor with respect yet show you are serious about getting paid. You should also call the debtor by his or her last name and show you are sincerely concerned about helping the debtor solve any problems. But don't let yourself get emotionally involved or let the debtor's excuse deflect your determination to get back the debt. Don't let a hard luck story throw you, even if true. Remember, the debtor still owes the money, and there are alternatives for finding a way to pay you other than making you wait.

If you do know the debtor, be friendly but firm. You want to preserve good feelings, but still show this is a serious call about the money that's due. Again, keep your emotional cool and preserve some distance. This is perhaps a little harder with a friend or a relative, but it can usually be done. Try to come across as more of a problem-solver who means business, rather than a friend who can be put off for a little longer while everyone else gets paid.

It's important to establish this rapport from the beginning of the conversation, because you only have a few seconds to make a good first impression and set the tone for the conversation. If you have never talked to the debtor before, your opening is especially important; the person will likely build an image of you immediately, and you want to make that first impression work to your advantage.

One way to establish rapport is to explain that you have had similar experiences, and can both understand and sympathize with the debtor. If the debtor thinks you are sincerely trying to help, he or she will be more likely to identify with you or be receptive to what you say.

For example, if you are one business owner talking to another business owner, you can discuss how you had to overcome debts yourself when you started out. If you are talking to someone having problems making ends meet, talk about the struggles you have had.

Whatever the situation, come in on the same wavelength as the debtor; make a sincere effort to show you understand.

The following sample conversation illustrates this approach.

> Debtor: I'm afraid I can't pay right now, since my debts have been so high the last few months. The factory I worked at closed a few months ago and I'm still unemployed.

> Creditor: Sure. I understand what it's like to be without a job, when you've worked at it so long. I had that experience, too, a few years ago, when my office closed, and I was out of work. But I found something part-time, and even though it wasn't exactly what I wanted, it made me feel really good to know I had a job and someone believed in me enough to give me another chance. I'll bet you could find something in your spare time, too, while you're looking for another regular job.

Stay in control of the conversation. Since you took the initiative in calling or in leaving a message to call you back, you're in charge. It's up to you to direct the call by having a goal for where you want the discussion to go and by setting the tone for the conversation.

In particular, you want to get paid as soon as possible and eliminate any barriers to that goal, so concentrate on achieving that end. If the debtor should try to deflect you from this goal, get the conversation back on track.

This is especially likely to happen if you call a friend or business associate. You mention the money, and suddenly your friend or colleague is saying something like: "Oh, yeah. That. Well, it's great to hear from you again. You know, our organization is planning a picnic for this Wednesday, and . . ."

If the debtor distracts you like this, simply acknowledge the comment (perhaps say something like: "Well, let's get into that later,") and get back to what you called about.

Avoid losing momentum by asking questions that give the debtor control of the conversation. For example, if the debtor expresses concern that he or she can't pay the whole amount due, don't ask, "Well, how much can you pay?" Then the debtor is likely to come back with an unreasonably low figure, which he or she thinks shows good faith. When you're negotiating from a low figure, it's hard to get back to what you want.

Instead, ask questions to establish what the debtor can pay if he or she acknowledges the debt. "How much time do you need to pay off the debt?" "How much are you short?" When the debtor responds, you are in a position to make an offer yourself.

Don't let yourself get emotional and lose control. It can be easy to get frustrated when you feel the debtor is delaying or giving you excuses. But stay cool.

You'll only make the situation worse by getting mad: you'll make the debtor more resistant to paying, and if you get abusive or threatening, you'll be treading on shaky legal ground. Besides, it's harder to think clearly and keep the conversation on track when you're emotional.

Conversely, if the debtor gets mad and yells at you, it's to your advantage to stay calm and collected, for the debtor will sense your confidence and control and will usually calm down.

If necessary, allow the debtor to get emotional and get out any anger or hostility. Sometimes debtors will get upset when you press them about the money they owe. Try not to take this personally. Often they are mad about their situation and are feeling generally frustrated, not just angry at you.

For example, if you are having trouble collecting and the debtor acknowledges the debt, it is likely he or she has other debts too. He or she may well be upset about being burdened with all these debts.

When you call, the debtor may want to express such feelings, and it is often advantageous to give the debtor the chance to let off steam. Just listen quietly. When the anger has dissipated, you can have a calm conversation. If you go into combat with the debtor or refuse to listen, it's likely you'll get the debtor madder--only now his or her anger isn't just general, but also directed at you.

Listen to what the debtor is saying so you can respond accordingly. When you listen, you have a chance to find out what the real problem is, learn about the debtor's true motivations, and understand what alternatives might be appropriate for resolving the situation.

Just as a good salesperson probes for information before trying to make a sale, so you should ask questions of the debtor and listen to the reply.

One of the worst things to do is to jump to conclusions and act on unwarranted assumptions about why the debtor can't or won't pay. You risk alienating the debtor further and reducing the chances the debtor will pay.

For example, in the following conversation, it is obvious the creditor hasn't listened:

> Debtor: I wish I could pay you for the TV I bought, but I don't have it now. I can barely pay the rent, and I've got lots of other bills.
>
> Creditor: I'm sorry. I've been waiting long enough. I can't wait any longer.
>
> Debtor: But I already told you. I don't have the money...

Instead, the creditor should try to show he or she understands the debtor and would like to help find a solution. For example, after the debtor states the problem, the creditor might say:

> Creditor: Well, I appreciate your concern in wanting to get this bill paid, and I realize you're having problems with your other bills. So I'd like to try to help you find a solution, especially since it's to your advantage to get your bills paid. You know, you might take out a loan so you can consolidate your debts, pay them all off, and then make a smaller payment each month on the loan. Or maybe we can work out a reasonable payment plan, if you can tell me how much time you need to pay off the balance.

Use pauses after you make a statement to give the debtor a chance to think and react. The goal here is to encourage the debtor to speak. Pausing after you say something, and waiting for the debtor to talk, is an excellent way to accomplish this.

One reason for pausing is that people feel uncomfortable with silences, so your silence puts pressure on the debtor to respond. You've said your piece, and it's up to the debtor to make the next move.

If the debtor hesitates or responds uncertainly, you may be

tempted to fill in the pauses and help out. Don't. Let the debtor respond and listen. For example, suppose you say, "You've gotten several reminders from us already, but we still haven't gotten your payment for the $200 balance. What seems to be the problem?"

You should wait until the debtor is clearly finished speaking, even if the debtor responds weakly ("Oh. Uh, well, I'm not really sure. I thought it was paid. Uh, well . . . perhaps you're right. Maybe I did forget to pay it after all.)"

Ask your questions in a positive way to encourage the debtor to say "yes"; then he or she is more likely to say "yes" when you ask for the money. The idea is to get the debtor used to agreeing with you. Then, he or she is more conditioned to continue agreeing when you ask for payment and will be more receptive if you suggest a few alternatives. You have gotten the debtor in a "yes" frame of mind with your questions.

For example, you might start off with a series of questions to which it is hard to say no, such as:

Creditor: Well, you do think of yourself as a responsible person, don't you?

Debtor: Yes.

Creditor: And you do value your reputation in the community, don't you?

Debtor: Yes.

Creditor: Then, don't you agree that it would be a good idea to pay off the money you owe our store, so you can keep your good credit record?

Debtor: Well, yes...

As you ask these questions, assume the debtor will answer positively, and your confidence will shine through. In turn, your confidence will make the debtor even more likely to say "yes."

Show you are positive and confident when you speak. Let the debtor know that you are sure the debt is owed and you can work out any problems that stand in the way of the debtor paying you. The advantage of this approach is that the debtor feels your certainty. This puts the burden on the debtor to dispute the debt. At the same time, you show you are convinced you can help the debtor solve any problems. Thus, you are in a better position to overcome objections, excuses, or stalls.

For example, if the debtor tries to put you off with a comment like, "Well, I'm sure this debt was already paid," you have a ready come-back you can say with confidence, such as, "I'm sorry, but my records don't show any payment. If you have a canceled check you can send me to support your claim, please send it along today. If not, I'll have to assume my records are valid, and I'll look forward to getting your payment by Friday."

Invite the debtor to get involved in finding a solution to the problem. This way you get his or her cooperation, and the debtor may think of solutions he or she hadn't thought of before. One advantage of getting the debtor involved is that he or she doesn't feel you have imposed the payment arrangement. If the debtor helps to come up with the solution, he or she has more of a commitment to keeping the bargain.

One way to get the debtor involved is to ask questions about what he or she thinks he should do. For example, "Since we're agreed on the balance that's due, how do you think you can get the money to pay this amount?"

If the debtor gets stuck, you can suggest several alternatives that the debtor may not have been aware of before. Then let the debtor select the alternative he or she prefers. For example, "Well, perhaps you could talk to your boss about an advance, or maybe your credit union would be willing to loan you some money. Your bank might give you a loan, or if you already have one, you can probably make arrangements with your bank to refinance it."

If the debtor says one alternative won't work, suggest another or ask the debtor for ideas.

If the debtor comes up with a stall, objection, grievance, or apparently phony excuse, be prepared to overcome it. We'll deal with the specifics about how to respond in the next chapters. You should have a rough idea of the kinds of responses you might get, though, so you can immediately counter an excuse with the proper response.

If the debtor stalls because he or she is uncertain about whether to acknowledge the debt or pay it, reassure the debtor the debt is due and that he or she should pay.

If the debtor raises an objection, be prepared to counter that objection and resell the debtor on paying the debt.

If there is a real grievance, be prepared to work out a way to resolve the complaint.

And if the debtor seems to be seeking to evade the debt with a phony excuse, be prepared to call the debtor on his actions and get to the real reason the debtor wants to evade the debt (he might think you're a sucker who will eventually go away if he stalls long enough). Then, when you talk, reaffirm what you expect the debtor to pay.

End your conversation with a specific action for the debtor to perform. Unless you decide that the debtor is a hopeless debt avoider and you need to take legal action or write the matter off, conclude your conversation with the debtor's agreement to do something. To get this agreement, emphasize that it's urgent for the debtor to act now, preferably the minute he or she hangs up the phone.

Though you may get a broken promise, and many bill collectors do, end the conversation on a positive note with an expectation that the debtor will act. If the promise is broken, you can deal with that later.

For now, however, assume the debtor is agreeing to act in good faith and ask the debtor to make a firm commitment.

Firm up the commitment to action with a dramatic statement or reminder of what the debtor has agreed to do. Once you have a commitment to act, go one step further to emphasize and reinforce it for the debtor. The practice effective bill collectors use, as recommended by the American Collectors Association, is to ask the debtor to write down what he or she has agreed to do and read it back.

For example, you might conclude your conversation thus:

> "Okay, then, Mrs. Allen, you've agreed to send us that check for $200 today. I'll be looking for it in the mail on Wednesday. So now, if you'll write down our address and the amount of the check . . . And now if you'll repeat that address and amount back to me, so you know you've got it right . . ."

CHAPTER 16:
Handling Stalls
and Objections

Stalls and objections occur when the debtor isn't ready or able to pay the bill or when he or she isn't sure whether to accept responsibility. The stall is basically an attempt to gain more time by delaying the date when the debtor has to assume responsibility for the bill or pay it; the objection is an excuse or reason why the debtor can't or won't pay. Sometimes the objection is based on a real dispute or grievance, something we'll deal with in a later chapter. But often the debtor raises an objection to try and get out of paying the bill altogether.

Since an individual with a real grievance is likely to respond as soon as the problem occurs (for example, if a recently purchased TV doesn't work, the person will call the store right away; if an order arrives damaged, the person will call to complain), you should treat objections involving a complaint with a good dose of skepticism. Perhaps you might respond by expressing your doubts that the dispute is really justified, or you might comment that it's unusually late to raise this argument. Often the debtor will respond by dropping the complaint, and you can treat the matter like a regular stall or objection. But if the debtor continues to complain, then deal with the matter as a real complaint.

The Right Attitude

Whenever you encounter a stall or objection or think a complaint may be a stall, take the attitude that the person owes the money and that you will overcome the problem so he or she will pay. It's easy to buy the debtor's excuses and become sympathetic; but remind yourself that it's your money. If you don't weaken, you can resell the debtor on paying you.

One way to look at objections is as a salesperson does: a request for more information. A prospect raises these objections to making a purchase because he or she doesn't have enough information to be sure. The salesperson seeks to overcome these objections by giving the prospect more details about how he or she will benefit from the product.

It's the same way in collecting debts. When an objection or stall arises, you want to give the debtor more information to reassure him or her that he or she owes the debt and that it is in the debtor's best interest to pay it.

Remember: unless the person raises a valid complaint, that person owes you the money and you expect him or her to pay. Be polite and courteous, but firm. You'd like to maintain good will, but you expect the person to pay.

Preparing to Respond

To respond effectively to a stall or objection, be prepared in advance by knowing   the kinds of objections people are likely to raise-- and how to answer them.

The types of objections will differ depending on whether you are dealing with an individual customer, business, or friend; on the type of debt (purchase or loan); and on other factors (such as the size of debt or business). But there are common objections that come up regularly. One good way to get prepared is to make a list of common excuses and how to respond. Sit down with a sheet of paper and brainstorm a list of excuses you have heard or are likely to hear, or keep a list of new excuses as you speak to debtors, so you'll be ready to respond when you hear that excuse again.)

Since a likely objection is that having no money, be aware of the various places the debtor can go to raise money. This way, you can turn someone else into the debtor's banker--not you.

The rest of this chapter lists some common stalls, objections, and possible responses; the next chapter describes some likely sources of money you can suggest.

Dealing with Stalls

The strategy for dealing with stalls is a little different from that of dealing with objections, since the stall is essentially a delaying tactic to put off acknowledging responsibility for the bill or to avoid paying it. The debtor isn't disputing the bill; he or she is playing for extra time. You have to reassure the staller that he or she is responsible, and that the problem can and must be handled now.

A good way to deal with any stall is to counter with an alternative, showing why the stall is not an important barrier to paying. Perhaps a debtor says he can't pay today: "My car is broken; I can't get out of the office." You come back with an alternative to derail the stall, such as, "You can send in your check by mail," or, "I'll be glad to stop by your office this afternoon."

In some cases the stall is a way to cover up or avoid expressing an objection. If so, try to uncover that. After you overcome a stall with an alternative, the debtor may suddenly reveal that there is another "real" reason that he or she doesn't want to pay or doesn't feel he or she should.

Say you tell a debtor she can send in a check if she can't stop by to see you, or you indicate you are willing to accept part of the balance if she doesn't have the whole thing. But the debtor really doesn't want to accept the responsibility for the bill and comes back with: "Well, to tell the truth, I don't think I owe the debt. I've had problems with the stereo ever since I bought it . . " Now you know the real reason the debtor is resisting and you must deal with that.

The following are some frequent stalls and good responses. You can create your own list of stalls and responses, too.

The debtor can't meet you to bring you the money. The debtor may come up with all kinds of reasons why it's impossible to meet you, such as, "I'm having trouble with the car," "I'm waiting for a package," or "I'm expecting someone to stop by."

The most effective response is to offer an alternative so the debtor doesn't have to meet you: "You can put your check in the mail today." "I'll stop by to pick your payment up." "I'll have someone from the office drop over."

The debtor has to check with someone else to see if the debt is valid or has already been paid. Typically, the individual consumer will say he or she has to check with a spouse, while the business debtor will have to go to a bookkeeper or accountant. But if your own records are up to date, you know when this is a stall.

A good strategy here is either to reassure the person that the debt is due (i.e., "We keep careful records, and we know we haven't received your payment"), or offer to call the person who needs to be contacted yourself so the debtor can't delay making the contact or use the excuse, when untrue, that this person says the bill is paid. When you do offer to call, the debtor will often realize the excuse won't work, won't want you to call yourself, and may counter with another reason, which might be the real one. For example, "Well, perhaps you're right and we didn't pay it. But we're a little slow with our payments this month, because we're short of cash."

The debtor has "already sent" you a check or money order, though it hasn't arrived. This is the old "the check is in the mail" or "you should have received the check" ploy. The debtor's strategy of trying to blame the mails may be good for a little time, but after a few days to give the debtor the benefit of the doubt, follow up if the check doesn't arrive. Ask questions to verify that the check was actually sent and suggest some of the following alternatives so you don't end up waiting for days for a check that doesn't come.

"When did you send your payment? Where did you send it from? Was it by check or money order? What was your check or money order number?" "Please send us another check. You can stop the first one, or we'll be glad to send it back." "We'll need a copy of the money order you sent. We'll be glad to help you trace it if it's lost." "Perhaps you think you mailed the check or money order. Please look around your office while we talk, and if you don't see it there, we'll need another check." "We'll wait until tomorrow, and if it doesn't arrive, we'll need you to make out another check and stop the first."

The debtor offers to put out a tracer to find out what happened to the payment he or she sent. This is another common ploy to buy time, akin to the "check is in the mail" story. If you go along with it, the debtor can go through the motions of tracing and have a few more weeks to play with your money. Commonly, the debtor will claim he or she has to trace it through the post office, which takes about 30 days to trace. If the debtor wants to stall a little longer, it's easy to add on a few more days on top of that.

One debtor, who eventually paid me when I took her to court, claimed she was tracing a money order through the post office to replace a bad check, which was already three weeks old when I got it back from the bank. By the time it became obvious that the post office wasn't going to find this mysterious missing document, the check was about two months old--well past the limits for criminal prosecution in the area (45 days), so my only remedies were civil. Before I finally realized the woman's game, I fell for still more stories: she lost the money order receipt; she would send another money order when she found it· a relative had inadvertently taken the new money order with her on vacation; etc.

So when you get a tracer story, don't get fooled. If you have any doubts, immediately put the burden on the debtor to show you documentation or give you a replacement, or be ready to take further action. You can even offer to help the debtor with the trace: "For our records, we'll need to have a copy within the next three days of the money order you say you sent us, so we can verify this as a trace." Or: "Even if you did send the money, we'll have to have a replacement check or money order while you trace it, and then when it turns up we'll return your original check." Or: "We'll be glad to help you trace down these funds, if you send us a copy of your money order. In the meantime, we'll need to have you issue another to us."

The debtor has sent you part of the money owed but owes more, and you have not agreed to partial payments. In this ploy to buy time, the debtor is hoping you'll let the matter slide, since he or she has sent in a partial payment suggesting good faith. Or the debtor may hope you make a mistake and think the bill is paid in full.

You should respond by writing or calling the debtor immediately. Thank him or her for the partial payment and restate your agreement about what the total amount due should be.

Then, if the debtor explains he or she doesn't have enough money, deal with this as you would any claim of insufficient funds.

The debtor claims that some business problem has prevented checking if the debt is valid or paid or that there has been a breakdown in the usual system for making payments. This is a convenient fiction for a business that is having cash flow problems and wants to buy time. Of course, this ploy may indicate that the company is hopelessly disorganized, in which case you can expect to have continuing problems collecting.

Some typical claims would include, "The computer is down," "We're short-handed," and "We're changing over in our accounting department, and we have some bugs in the new system." There are probably as many potential variations on the basic technique as there are companies.

When you get an excuse about administrative difficulties, you should expect any problem to be a short-term one, lasting only a few days at most. Computer problems usually last only a few hours. There is no good reason these administrative foul-ups should affect a payment that is long overdue (probably about six to eight weeks at this point). And if the debtor talks about a confused record system, this suggests a deeper problem.

Show you are not willing to accept any of these excuses for continued delay and counter with questions like the following so you can deal with the real problem.

"How long has the computer been down? When is it going to be fixed?" "Why should a computer breakdown, which only lasts a few hours or days, delay payment by several weeks (or months)?" "If you are having so many problems with your computer, why can't you handle this by hand?" "How short-handed are you? What sort of employees do you need? What are you doing to correct this problem? Why should the absence of these workers (if they have nothing to do with making payments) affect you paying the money you owe?" "How are you changing your system? What kind of bugs? Why can't you pay me using the old system and use the new system when you get it organized?" "How long have you been having these problems with your records? What are you doing to get them straightened out? "If you have such serious problems with your records, you may not be able to find out the information you want; so you can go by our records instead, and these show you haven't paid. Shall we do that?"

The debtor claims the person who pays the bills is unavailable. This is a common business excuse. Some variations on the theme include, "Our bookkeeper is on vacation," "We're waiting for a signature," and "The person who usually pays the bills is sick."

Again, check out the information to make sure this isn't a convenient excuse to delay. Sometimes, when you put pressure on the debtor, you'll find that someone else can fill in for the bookkeeper or that the needed signature can easily be found. And if the debtor says that someone is sick, your reaction depends on whether it's a serious matter like a heart attack or something routine like a cold. Get the answers you need by asking appropriate questions.

"When is the bookkeeper (or other person who pays the bills) returning? Can someone else take care of this matter in the meantime?" "Whose signature is needed? Can you take care of this matter without that signature? Why not?" "What's wrong with the person who is sick? Can someone else do his or her job?"

Or perhaps make this offer: "I'll be glad to speak to the person whose signature is needed myself."

The debtor claims the bill was turned over to someone else to pay and that person should have sent it. Perhaps the debtor did turn over the bill to someone else, believes he or she did, or is just making an excuse. To find out, ask for more information about who is supposed to pay; then offer to check up to make sure this person knows he or she is supposed to pay and will do it.

"Who did you give the bill to?" "When did you do this?" "When did they say they would pay it?" "If this other person is going to be paying us, let me call and check myself. What's the number?" (If you are dealing with a stall, the debtor will often stop you from asking more questions at this point, admit he or she may not have referred the bill after all, or agree to send you the money. If it's clear that you are not put off easily, the debtor is more likely to address the real problem.)

The debtor claims he or she has been too busy to get around to paying you and is still very busy. Perhaps the debtor is in fact busy, but this is no excuse. If he or she thought the debt was important enough, he or she would take care of it. So you want to make the debtor understand that the debt is a matter of priority. In addition, point out that he or she can take care of the matter in short order.

"Sure, we're very busy here, too. But we make sure we get everything that's important done. And this debt is important, because (and give a few reasons: the debtor could lose his or her good credit status, you will hold up an order the debtor has already placed, future business between you will be jeopardized, etc.)" "I'm sure if your car broke down, you would get it fixed right away, even though you're busy. Well, this matter is just as important, because . . ." "I can understand how this could be an oversight. But you can take care of this in a few minutes. While we're on the phone, all you have to do is take out your checkbook, write us a check, and put it in the mail."

The debtor claims there is no time to pay the bills now because of special circumstances. This is a variation on the "I'm too busy to pay" theme, though in this case, the debtor is claiming company-wide circumstances are responsible. The possibilities are endless. "We're planning a gala party, and all our efforts are going into that." "It's time for our fiscal year audit, and we don't have time to pay our bills now." "The auditors are in." "We're involved in a legal battle, and that's taking all of our time."

Here the best response is again to stress the urgency of the situation and show that it's to the debtor's benefit to pay you, even though the company may be very busy now. If the firm wants to keep doing business with you, that gives you some clout. Or perhaps you can come up with a suggestion to reduce the company's time problem, such as suggesting how the company can organize its activities more efficiently.

The debtor is experiencing some major changes in his or her business--a change in partners; new officers or managers; a purchase by another company, etc. When a business change has occurred or is expected to occur soon, a businessperson will frequently delay making payments so that the debt may be taken over by the future owners, or because the changed environment is a good excuse to put off paying bills thereby improving cash flow.

In this situation, you must act quickly to determine who is really responsible for the debt, the individual personally or the business; then decide what to do on that basis.

If the person has signed a personal note guaranteeing your credit, both that person and the business are responsible, and even if the person leaves, he or she remains responsible if the new owner doesn't pay. If the person leaving has no responsibility, perhaps you can convince him or her that it's an advantage to get past obligations paid to promote a smooth transition. If you can't do this, speak to the new owners or management as soon as possible to introduce yourself as someone they will want to continue working with, so they will see that it is to their advantage to pay the bill.

In any case, when a business is transferred from one party to another and there are any past debts in the name of the business, the obligation remains with the business. Sometimes the new owners may try to get out of this. If they do, simply tell them you know the law.

I once discovered that a newspaper had reprinted, without permission, a substantial number of marketing tips from my copyrighted book. In the same issue, the paper announced a change of ownership. I wrote to the new owner asserting my claim and requesting compensation. The owner argued that the article in question was the responsibility of the previous editor--but of course the new owner was himself liable, for in taking over the business, he had assumed all of its obligations and liabilities. Eventually a compromise was worked out allowing me approximately $1500 worth of advertising in his newspaper--roughly equivalent to the amount I would have been paid to write an article of the same length as the extract in question.

So don't let a change in business arrangements work to your disadvantage. Find out at once who is responsible and let the debtor know you know. Then try to work out arrangements to maintain good will--but be ready to get tough, if necessary, to assert your rights.

The debtor has had an illness, accident, or family problems interfering with his or her ability to pay. In some cases personal excuses are used as a delaying tactic; in other cases they are real difficulties resulting in a serious financial problem. Ask more questions to find out if this is a real objection or another excuse. Or, if someone else in the family is having the problem, the question arises: why should this interfere with the payment of your debt?

"Who is ill? Your spouse? Your children? If you're not ill yourself, why is this creating problems for you in paying the bill?" "How long have you been out of work?" "How has this illness affected your business?" "How much longer do you expect to be off work (or away from your business)?" "Are you getting any sick pay or disability insurance?" "Do you have accident or health insurance?" "Have you filed a claim? Do you need any help in filing?" "When can you pay the balance due?" (Or: "When can you start making regular payments again?")

If it looks like the debtor really has had a serious problem because of illness or a major business calamity (like a fire, flood, or very large decline in business), be sympathetic and agree to delay. At the same time, make sure the debtor still acknowledges owing the money and will keep in touch with you regularly about when he or she can start paying again. After all, you do want to be understanding, but you don't want the debtor to think of your debt as a charity contribution. You expect the debtor to get back on his or her feet or get the business going again; then you expect to start receiving your money.

The debtor is going through a separation or a divorce. Sometimes a debtor experiencing marital problems will seek delay, because of emotional turmoil. In other cases the situation may be causing financial difficulties, or the debtor may expect the other spouse to pay, especially if he or she took on this debt because of the other spouse.

If you encounter this situation, first get more information about the legal status of the relationship and the debt. If the debtor signed an agreement or made the arrangement with you, he or she is still responsible and you should mention that fact. On the other hand, an ex-spouse will no longer be responsible for the individual debts of the other.

As in the case of illness, accident, or family problems, be sympathetic and supportive, but remember, the debtor owes you the money and you're not to blame for the divorce--so you shouldn't have to wait an excessive amount of time for your money or have the debtor try to escape the debt.

If you can, get any current information on new addresses, new jobs, and so forth, so that if you have to follow up legally later, you will have this data.

"When did the legal separation occur? Where? Who are the attorneys handling the case?" "Is there any change in your current employer or business situation? If so, where can you be reached? Where does your spouse work?" "Do you need some help in finding other sources of money now?"

The debtor makes a promise and then breaks it. Generally, when the debtor makes a promise to send you money and breaks it, he or she isn't fully sold on paying the debt or feels he or she can't afford it. Your job is to reconvince the person to pay or suggest alternate sources of money.

If you have to persuade the debtor, you might stress that the debtor made an agreement with you, that you accepted his or her word or were trying to do a favor in accepting the payment arrangements you did, and that you feel it is important to keep promises because they represent a commitment. You might also ask why the debtor didn't let you know if he or she couldn't keep the commitment and say you are willing to make one last agreement. But stress that you want to be sure the debtor can handle any agreement you reach, and that you expect him or her to keep the bargain or that's it--you're going to get tough. (Then, if necessary, do.)

If you don't already have a promissory note, this is a good time to ask for one to get the debtor to reaffirm the debt.

"Why didn't you let me know if you couldn't pay me as you promised?" "I thought you were going to send me your check, but I never received it. Why didn't you send it as agreed?" "I trusted you to keep your commitment when we made our agreement. Don't you want me to continue to think of you as a trustworthy person?" "If I make another agreement with you, I want to be sure you understand this is the last one I will make before I take further action." "I'd like to work out another arrangement, but I want to be sure it's a promise you can keep, because I'm going to take further action if you don't." "Just to be sure there aren't any more misunderstandings, I'd like to sign a promissory note with you indicating the total amount due and how much you are going to pay me each month." "In the future, I want to be sure you understand our agreement." (Then set the payment date; amount; whether check, money order or cash; and whether the person is going to mail in the money or give it to you in person.)

Then, of course, there's the last stand. "Since you weren't willing to make the payments we agreed on, I'd like to get the full payment that's due today. Otherwise I will have to take further action."

There are all sorts of possibilities after a broken promise, depending on the nature and size of the debt and your relationship to the debtor. What's important is to be firm in setting up a new agreement, reestablish the person's agreement to pay the debt, and, if you can, get the new agreement in writing. Should the debtor break the promise again without an acceptable explanation, it's time to get tough.

The debtor is trying to avoid talking to you or is avoiding your correspondence. If the debtor is trying to avoid you, things are probably a bit more serious than you thought. When this happens, the debtor is typically trying to avoid other people, too, because he or she has financial problems and either can't afford to pay or doesn't want to. In some cases, the debtor wants to avoid you because he or she is embarrassed to discuss the situation, or may not want to surface until after the problem is resolved. Then, too, a debtor may hope that if the avoidance game goes on long enough, you will forget about the whole situation.

If the debt is small enough, you may want to write it off as more trouble than it's worth. Some creditors, however, as a matter of principle, never give up.

In any case, look for early warning signs that the debtor is avoiding you and be ready to act quickly to deal with the situation, before the debtor disappears permanently and your chances of getting paid become nil.

Some early warning signs include the following.

Your mail is returned marked "not here" or "moved," or it's forwarded to an address that isn't any good and then returned--and you don't think the debtor has moved. (Sometimes the debtor will forward his or her own mail in this way to persuade creditors he or she has gone, but may still be there.)

The debtor doesn't return your calls, although you leave many messages.

The debtor suddenly starts screening his or her own calls or has people in the office do the same. In some large companies secretaries screen calls as a matter of course, so the boss only speaks to the people he or she approves. But in a small company, where things are more informal and people usually answer their own calls, this screening is often a warning, particularly if the debtor also won't take or return your calls. It suggests he or she is trying to avoid creditors.

The debtor never seems to answer a personal phone, though you call often at different times of the day and at times get a busy signal. This usually means the debtor has decided not to answer the phone, though he or she may still be using it. If the situation worsens, the debtor may soon have the phone disconnected. (You may encounter a permanently switched-on answering machine as part of the same syndrome.)

The debtor is always out or in conference when you call, and doesn't call you back. Some businesspeople are very busy or want to give that impression to seem important. But debtors can use this excuse conveniently, as well, to evade and delay creditors.

The debtor won't accept certified letters and they come back to you. People with financial problems often do this because they imagine these letters probably threaten legal action or include court appearance documents--and they are often right.

The debtor has recently taken some actions that suggest he or she is getting ready to move or go out of business, such as leaving an apartment, selling furniture, getting rid of an answering service, closing a business, or reducing the employee ranks to a skeleton staff. Another sign of impending doom is that the debtor has been very unsuccessful in some important effort, ranging from getting a job to selling a product line or staging a successful event.

You discover that the debtor is suddenly being hit with a number of complaints or legal suits from other creditors.

What do you do if you are confronted with any of these situations? Act quickly. Find a way to confront the debtor to learn what is going on, or take some immediate action to file suit and serve the debtor while he or she is still around. The debtor may be on the verge of giving up and disappearing, if things have gotten so bad that there appear to be no other alternatives.

I did both before that travel promoter I was working for skipped town. He had been avoiding calls from me and many other people, and I left a series of messages with his receptionist about my plans to come in when he was in the office. Through her, I finally found a time when he would be there, appeared, and persuaded him to give me a partial reimbursement check. Then I listened while he explained his plans to reimburse me and other creditors after a big party he was throwing the following month.

Since I suspected the event might be a disaster because of inadequate planning and publicity, I filed a small claims complaint and attended the party with a friend who would serve the papers if I felt there was no hope of collecting otherwise. When it became apparent the party was not going to break even, I had my friend serve the papers. And a few days later, the promoter left town.

Of course, you still have to go to court and collect on your judgment in such a case. But following the approach I did at least left that avenue open. The creditors who waited lost their chance to serve the promoter before he left, so their attempts to collect later if and when the man surfaces and has money again will be that much more difficult. They still have to go through the process of serving him and trying the case in court.

CHAPTER 17:
Dealing with Objections

The objection differs from the stall, since it represents a real reason the debtor thinks payment is impossible or inappropriate. The debtor is not trying to delay giving you the reason and is not trying to avoid the issue. Rather, the debtor accepts the debt or at least part of it, but objects to paying it now for some reason.

This reason is commonly some variation on the problem of not having enough money, although the debtor may also claim that someone else has assumed the responsibility to pay. As in the stall, your job is to counter each objection. If the problem is money, learn more about the situation, continue to press for payment, and suggest some sources of funds the debtor can use so you don't continue to play banker.

In some cases the debtor may express a grievance to conceal an objection. Your strategy should be the same as with stalls: probe to find out more about the grievance. If it doesn't have real substance, look for the underlying objection and deal with that.

The Debtor Claims Payment Is Impossible Because of Financial Problems

There are numerous variations on this theme, but the core problem is that the debtor claims to be having financial difficulties. It is important to understand why, because then you can find out if the debtor's claims are true, how serious the problem is, what options the debtor has to raise money, and whether you can help. The answer will also help you to decide whether to agree to wait, arrange a payment plan, or press for your money now.

Certainly, you should be sympathetic and supportive if the situation warrants; but don't let the debtor's pleas for patience or sympathy blind you to the fact that you are owed money. Some of the common claims involving money problems and suggested ways to react to them are outlined below.

The Debtor Claims to Owe Many Other People Money, Too

Frequently debtors with financial problems will complain about all the other people they owe, hoping you will become more docile in seeking your money since you are one of the crowd. Or they may ask, "The other creditors are being understanding and waiting; why can't you?"

The main questions to ask yourself before deciding how to respond are these: Why are there so many other creditors? And why are they willing to wait, if this is true? If this is a special calamity case (such as a business or individual encountering some unusual and unexpected reverses) pull back and be patient. The debtor will pay when he or she recovers, and will appreciate your understanding and concern.

But if the debtor has been irresponsible--or if a business has been taking unwarranted risks or is being run into the ground by incompetent managers--consider the excuse a ploy to buy time. Take action now before it is too late.

If you discover you are in a rapidly deteriorating situation of diminishing resources, you have to act fast, because it's likely that only some of the creditors, if any, are going to be paid. So you want to step up the pressure to be one of the first in line.

To decide what to do, here are some questions to raise.

Why does the debtor owe other creditors? Who are they and how much are they owed? How long has the debtor had a problem in paying off creditors? Has there been any unexpected problem (like a personal tragedy or business disaster) that warrants sympathy and support for the debtor? What does the debtor plan to do to pay off creditors? Does the debtor seem to be sincere in proposing this plan? Is there anything you can do to encourage the debtor to pay you off first, or to pay you more than the other creditors? For example, can you do something to help the debtor, or do you have anything the debtor might want? Has the debtor considered other sources of funding to get the money to pay off his creditors?

The Debtor Claims to Be Only Making Enough to Pay Basic Expenses

You are most likely to get this excuse from an entrepreneur who is trying to make it, or from a person who likes to live a little beyond his or her means.

The question to raise here is whether the debtor is ever likely to make more than this basic budget. Perhaps he or she has unrealistic expectations of success and should be willing to cut back on some so-called "basics" to pay the bills.

To find out, confront the debtor. Ask questions to learn if he or she really intends or is likely to pay in the near future, and decide if further action is needed based on the debtor's response.

What are the debtor's basic expenses? What can the debtor do to increase his or her income to pay off debts? How likely is this? How soon is this apt to happen? Can the debtor reduce some expenses to pay you back? If not, why not? After all, why should you subsidize the debtor's business or lifestyle? Is there any way you can help the debtor make more money? What other sources of funds has the debtor considered to raise money? Is he or she willing to use them?

The Debtor Claims He/She Can't Pay Because of Losing a Job or Business Difficulties

Sometimes this argument is a delaying tactic, but in other cases the debtor has intended to pay, but now feels he or she can't. Your approach here should be to determine how serious the problem is, whether the debtor is sincerely trying to resolve it or using it to discourage creditors, and how the problem affects the debtor's ability to pay. For example, the debtor might have other sources of income, be able to borrow, or have likely prospects for a new job or business. Then, use this information to determine if the debtor can pay you now and how much.

Ask: why has the debtor left his job and where was he or she working? How long has this situation been a problem? What has the debtor been doing to find work or resolve the business problem?

You might suggest ideas to help the debtor. If the debtor isn't responsive, he or she may have a bad attitude or have become discouraged. Nevertheless, it may be worthwhile to inquire in this area.

What other sources of income does the debtor have? Does the debtor have any unemployment insurance coming and can he or she pay you anything out of this? How much and when? Will the debtor be getting any back pay? What are the debtor's prospects for a new job or getting another business going? How soon is this likely to be a source of income to pay off your debt? Can the debtor get some financial assistance from relatives or friends? Does the debtor's spouse work? Where? If so, you can tap this source of income. If you conclude the debtor really can't pay you back now, get him or her to promise to let you know when things change. But also plan to follow up yourself, since many debtors with job or business problems won't call.

The Debtor Claims He/She Can't Pay Because of an Illness or Personal Family Problems

Again, this argument may be a delaying tactic, as described earlier, or it may be a real objection. If so, determine how seriously this problem affects the debtor's ability to pay. For example, if the debtor is ill, his or her income may be seriously curtailed. If a spouse, child, or other relative is ill, the debtor may be worried about paying medical bills, but still have enough to pay you (or perhaps the doctor bills can wait). The debtor may have enough insurance to cover any medical bills and pay you besides.

So, again, ask questions to assess the situation and decide if the debtor can and should pay.

Is the debtor or someone else in the family ill? If someone else, why should this hold up the debtor's payments to you? And is the debtor justified in not paying your debt now under the circumstances? If the debtor is ill, how serious is the illness? How long has he or she been away from work, and how much longer is this likely to continue? And where does the debtor work? Does the debtor receive payments while ill, such as sick pay or disability insurance? Or is the debtor likely to receive a lump sum settlement later on through medical or accident insurance? (If necessary, advise the debtor how to file a claim.)

If it seems the debtor can't pay for awhile, you might suggest sources of money or ask the debtor to agree to start paying you by a certain date. In any case, ask the debtor to call you to let you know how things are going. If you don't hear from the debtor, call every few weeks.

The Debtor is Considering Bankruptcy

Sometimes a debtor may claim to be near bankruptcy to buy time or persuade a creditor to disappear. In other cases, the threat of bankruptcy is quite real, and further pressure from you could send the debtor over the brink.

You need to get information to assess the seriousness of the situation and decide what to do. If the debtor is almost at the point of bankruptcy, it's probably best to back off from collecting any money immediately. However, you can try to make your situation more secure by having the debtor give you a secured note against some personal or business property. The advantage of doing this is that if the debtor merely owes you money, you will be treated like all the other creditors, and any unsecured assets, over and above those that are exempt, will be distributed among all creditors on an equal proportional basis. However, if you have a written agreement giving you certain items of property not assigned to anyone else, you will usually end up with those items as long as you receive the note over three months before the debtor files. (If you get the note within this three-month period, you may run into problems. The bankruptcy laws state that a person planning a bankruptcy cannot give away assets in such a way as to favor one creditor over another. This means anything the debtor gives up during this three-month pre-bankruptcy period usually has to be returned to the bankruptcy estate to be distributed to creditors.)

If the debtor has a struggling business and wants to keep doing business with you in the hope of saving it, another strategy is to persuade the owner to sign a personal note to guarantee any money due to you--including both past and future credit.

Still another possibility, if you are dealing with a business, is to contact the other creditors to see if you can collectively hold off forcing the debtor into bankruptcy so the debtor can sell the business. Even if the resources of the business are liquidated to pay off creditors, you'll get more from the sale of a going business than one where the business has gone bankrupt.

What kinds of questions should you ask in assessing a near-bankruptcy situation? There are a number of topics to address.

How long has the debtor been considering a bankruptcy? How close is the debtor to filing? Has the possibility of bankruptcy been discussed with anyone? Does the debtor plan to get a lawyer? How many other creditors does the debtor have? How much is owed? What can you, as a creditor, do to help the person avoid bankruptcy? Will the debtor give you a secured note for some of your property (merchandise, inventory, etc.) if you offer additional credit? (This may sound like a terrible idea, because you are giving the person more money and therefore "throwing good money after bad." But in fact you are in a better position with a $2,000 secured note than with $1,000 in unsecured credit. In the first case you'll get it all, if the individual or business goes under. In the latter case you'll probably only receive a tiny percentage on the dollar if this collapse occurs.)

The Debtor Claims He or She Has Filed for Bankruptcy

If the debtor does file, you're faced with a fait accompli and should forget about making additional routine collection efforts, since the courts are now involved. But there are still some things you can do to improve your situation.

First, verify that the individual or business has filed by getting the date of the bankruptcy and the number. If the debtor has not filed, treat the matter as a "considering bankruptcy" situation.

Next (if this is an individual bankruptcy) find out why the individual went bankrupt and what's likely to be left after the individual deducts the exemptions allowed by federal or state law. These usually amount to about $8,000. Also, find out how much is owed to all the claimed creditors, and ask if the debtor has listed you as a creditor. Determine if the amount on the records is as much as you think you should get. If it is less than expected, try to get the debtor to correct this. Alternatively, you can contest this claim with the bankruptcy judge.

If the debtor has listed you, you can get a rough idea of how much you will receive on the dollar owed by dividing the total amount available by the amount owed to all creditors. If the debtor hasn't listed you, he or she may still owe you the full debt--though you probably shouldn't expect payment for some time while the debtor gets back on his or her feet.

If you've got a secured note, verify that the secured property is still available and remind the debtor that he or she has to keep this because it belongs to you. If you can, get a new note restating this obligation to further remind the debtor.

If you don't have a secured note, try to get the debtor to reaffirm your debt. This means that even if you have been listed as a creditor, the debtor has agreed to pay and can't discharge your debt. Not all debtors are going to want to do this--after all, the purpose of a bankruptcy is to get rid of debts. But you may be able to convince the debtor it's to his or her advantage. For example, you might suggest ways you can help the debtor (such as providing new credit after the bankruptcy or giving a good reference or referral to a job). If you can't get the debtor to reaffirm the whole debt, perhaps you can compromise on a partial figure. Then, assuming the bankruptcy judge approves (which is usually the case if it can be shown that the debtor has acted knowingly and voluntarily) the debtor will still owe you the debt.

If the debtor is involved in a business bankruptcy, again, you should try to find out the reason for the bankruptcy and learn how much is likely to be left after liabilities are deducted from assets. In this case, be sure you are listed as a creditor; if not, apply to the courts by filing a Proof of Claim. Otherwise, if you're not listed and your debt is with a business (and is not guaranteed by the owners), when the business is liquidated, you're out of luck.

As in the individual case, verify that any secured property owed to you is on hand and make sure the owner doesn't dispose of it.

If you have had a good relationship with the owner or think he or she might start a new business and want to do business with you, you might try to get the owner to agree to pay your debt personally. Admittedly, this approach is often a long shot. But if what you offer is valuable enough to the debtor (i.e., special contacts, or products the debtor will want but can't easily get elsewhere), the owner just may do it. At least it doesn't hurt to try.

The Debtor Claims to Have Longer Payment Arrangements than You Expected or Agreed Upon

This kind of objection shouldn't come up if your financial policies and agreements with customers or clients are already established, clearly stated, and mutually agreed upon in the first place. This problem sometimes arises if you haven't made your own policy clear, if it is different from traditional payment standards in your industry, or if there has been a misunderstanding about payment terms.

You might expect your customer to pay when you deliver the work, while your customer expects to pay after you send your bill. You might expect to get paid as soon as your client gets the invoice, while your client thinks he or she has 30 days. Your terms might be payment in 30 days, but your customer might usually have a 45-60 day arrangement. You might expect to get paid based on the date you receive the order, while your customer counts the time from when he or she receives the goods.

To deal with a length of payment objection, you have to go back to your original written agreement, if any, to see what you agreed. Before insisting on your own terms for payment, consider the risks of antagonizing the customer or client and decide how much you want to continue to deal with this person. For example, if your terms aren't clearly stated in a contract or invoice signed by your customer, you are probably stuck with your client's or customer's usual payment schedule, which may be longer than your expected terms. Even if you do have a contract stating that your terms are payment within 30 days, you may want to make an exception for a big company that pays in 45 to 60 days. (Big companies typically do take longer to pay, but you can usually count on them paying you.)

On the other hand, when your agreement is clear and you feel your customer or client needs you, you can take a stronger position and say something like, "Even if your company usually pays other creditors between 45-60 days, our agreement was for 30 days, and that's when we expect to be paid."

It's a good idea to work out your own policies for dealing with this claim in advance. Then you are better prepared to negotiate terms.

The Debtor Claims that an Error in Processing Your Bill Has Delayed Payment

This is a common objection made by businesspeople. It might be a real objection due to some goof, or it might be a stall. If the claim seems to be a real objection, deal with the problem in good faith to get it corrected; then follow up to make sure the matter is being taken care of. If, after a week or so, you see that nothing is happening, you can suspect a stall, probably because the business is having cash-flow problems.

Some typical difficulties delaying payment might include those listed below.

"The purchase order has the incorrect number and doesn't match the shipment bill." "We need a proof of delivery." "The invoice was kept by the purchasing department and wasn't sent over for payment." "The original invoice was misplaced, and we didn't know it until you called." "There was a pricing discrepancy, so we were holding the invoice until we could find out the correct price."

In response to any of these objections, ask additional questions to find out what the debtor needs and, if the request is reasonable, supply it. For example, send a new purchase order or invoice or a duplicate contract listing the agreed-upon price. Include a request for immediate payment with whatever you send.

If the debtor doesn't respond in the next week or two, unless he or she has apparently legitimate reasons (such as having to send requests for payment through the usual channels in a large company) treat the matter as a stall and look for the real objection, so you can act accordingly.

The Debtor Claims that Someone Else is Responsible for Paying the Bill

An individual debtor who owes money is apt to claim that someone else is responsible when he or she thinks some institution or organization is picking up the bill. For example, the debtor may claim it's up to the insurance company, credit union, or employer to pay.

With a business, such a claim may occur when there are internal problems and the chains of command aren't clear. Someone may make an unauthorized purchase and later try to pass the responsibility to another person. Or a new owner may try to disavow responsibility for what went on before.

To deal with these objections, you first have to pinpoint who really is responsible. In some cases, if arrangements have been made, an individual simply has to sign for something and the company's insurance company, credit union, or employer will pick up the bill. Often, however, the individual has to pay first and afterwards file the necessary forms to get reimbursed. The debtor may not want to be bothered, or may simply forget. So, when the bills arrive, he or she may not realize this, and may get mad and refuse to pay.

I sat in on a court case like this. A woman had correctly filed her first few claim forms after an industrial accident, and the insurance company sent its payment directly to the doctor. Then she got busy, lost the papers, and never filed the additional claims. When the doctor came after her for his money, she told him she didn't owe it, and that her insurance company should pay. But by now it was too late: the deadline for filing had passed. She kept insisting she wouldn't pay, and finally the doctor had to win his case in court.

You can avoid getting stuck by someone's mistaken attempt to pass along responsibility for a debt by finding out who is really responsible as soon as a debtor makes this claim. If you don't already have an agreement with the organization the debtor claims is responsible, the debtor is probably supposed to pay and get reimbursed.

If possible, clarify this situation with the debtor before you make any arrangements to provide services or extend credit so you can, if necessary, make your agreement with a different, responsible party. If you haven't done this, act as soon as there is a payment problem to reaffirm that your agreement is with the debtor and the debtor has to collect from the other party. If the debtor isn't sure what to do, help, if you can, by suggesting where the debtor can get forms. You can even assist the debtor in filling them out.

If you are dealing with a business, do some research to determine who is responsible and talk to that person yourself. Don't leave it up to the debtor only or you may be waiting a long time. If you are in the classic buck-passing situation, where the person who made a purchase or arranged for a service claims the boss or department head is responsible, talk to the boss or department head. If he or she returns the buck to the employee, saying the employee made the agreement on his or her own, you may have to go to the next level to find out what company policies are in a case like this. If so, tell the employee or boss or both what you intend to do. At this point, they may prefer to work out some agreement themselves to resolve the matter before you get the whole company involved and jobs possibly end up on the line.

In most cases involving a new owner, your debt with the old company will be passed along to him, unless you had a special personal deal with the prior owner. All business liabilities and assets stay with the business.

Contact the new owner about the debt, and if he or she resists, use the stick-and-carrot approach. Point out that you would like to continue doing business together and that you can be helpful to the new owner, but make it clear that he or she is responsible for the debt in taking over the business.

If the old owner personally guaranteed the debt, responsibility for the debt still falls on him or her, too. But use that only for backup, if you have to go to court to collect. It's more appropriate to try to collect from the new owner, who has taken over what presumably will continue to be a going, successful enterprise.

The Debtor Has Died

When you call or write and someone tells you that the debtor has died, your first response should be to be sympathetic and understanding. Do not make any immediate collection efforts or assume that you are being lied to; however, be aware that some debtors trying to avoid creditors may use this as a story, hoping the creditor will go away.

In any case, ask for the date and place of death. If the death occurred within the past two weeks (and assuming you have no reason to believe you are being given a line), simply thank the person who gave you this information and ask who will be handling the debtor's affairs.

If your bill is a personal matter, you want the name and address of the administrator or attorney for the estate. If there is no estate, ask if there is life insurance. Get the name of the company handling this policy so you can find out how much insurance there is and who the beneficiaries are. With this information you can file a Creditor's Claim against the estate or seek payment from the beneficiaries. The only other possibility for collecting if a debtor dies without any money or a policy is to look for a relative who might feel a moral obligation to pay off the debts. This is not much more than a long shot, but you may want to try anyway at an appropriate time.

If your bill is based on a business arrangement, find out who is taking over the debtor's business affairs. (These will usually be passed on to the debtor's partners or anyone taking over the business.)   If the debtor has made the agreement on behalf of a large business, you may get paid as you normally would, since business is apt to continue as usual. However, if the agreement was made recently, you may have to struggle to get the debtor's successor to accept the agreement and the debt. If you think there might be any problem of this sort, act quickly to firm things up.

Once you have the name of the appropriate person to contact, use your judgment and sensitivity in deciding how and when to follow up. Remember, it's usually fitting to wait at least two weeks after the death to ask for payment. This way you show the proper respect and won't offend the debtor's relatives or business associates as a heartless creditor. And if you hope for continued business with the debtor's firm, you certainly want to be diplomatic.

CHAPTER 18:
Helping the Debtor to Find Money

Many debtors say they can't pay because they don't have the money. (At least they think they don't). So one way to increase your chances of getting paid is to help the debtor find the money.

The technique works with debtors who are trying to stall you, as well as with those who really are having financial woes. In the case of the stall, the debtor realizes you're not going to be put off by an easy excuse, and your suggestions may wear down resistance. Alternatively, if the debtor is really in financial trouble, your suggestions can improve the situation to such a degree that you end up getting paid. Moreover, by helping the debtor, you increase his or her incentive to pay in gratitude for your help.

Most of the following money sources are open both to the debtor with personal debts and to the debtor with a small business that's in trouble, though some are more appropriate for the individual debtor only. The first group of sources are places where the debtor can usually obtain enough money to pay you in full. The second set of sources are most appropriate if the debtor is going to be spacing out payments to you. You may have additional suggestions of your own.

When you mention some of these money sources, the debtor may resist. There is a feeling of security associated with having those funds and many people won't want to tap them to pay you. For example, the debtor may not want to touch savings or sell stocks. He or she may not want to contact other people, such as friends, relatives, or a boss, for a loan, because, in the debtor's view, this only means taking on more obligations and, worse, these obligations will involve family and/or personal contacts.

When you hit these obstacles, the best strategy is first to suggest some alternatives that might be more acceptable to the debtor. Say the debtor doesn't want to touch his savings or ask his friends to loan money. You might recommend he take out a bank loan or sell some property. If the debtor repeatedly turns down your suggestions, ask what other sources he or she might suggest. This is a good technique to get the debtor involved in the problem-solving process and thereby promotes cooperation. However, if you feel you are stalemated because the debtor has turned down everything and has no ideas of his or her own, be sympathetic but firm, stressing that the debtor has owed the debt to you for some time so it's only fair you be paid.

Sources of Funds for Making Major Payments

Checking and savings accounts. Professional bill collectors usually recommend this source first, since it's the easiest place for the debtor to get money quickly. You might assume the debtor doesn't have any money in the bank. (Otherwise, why claim to be broke?)   But often debtors are simply reluctant to draw funds because they don't want to deplete their reserves. They feel they should pay their debts out of any surplus.

If such issues come up, you should emphasize the importance of paying off the bill, using the usual appeals (continued good credit or further business together). You might remind the debtor that after he or she pays you off, the account can easily be built up again.

Stocks and bonds. Many debtors have these, although they may not think of these certificates as a source of ready cash. In fact, debtors sometimes forget they have these resources locked away; or they may not know a bond has matured and can be cashed in.

Here again, you may run into debtor reluctance, since the stocks or bonds may provide a feeling of security. Besides using the usual appeals, one strategy is to suggest that the debtor keep the stocks and use them as collateral or take out a loan. Then you can be paid out of the proceeds.

Another alternative, if you've got some gambling spirit, is to suggest the debtor sign over to you a stock worth about the same amount as the debt. Then, if payment is made to you by a certain date, you return the stock; otherwise you keep it (and if the stock goes up in price, you may even make some money).

Income tax refund. This suggestion obviously works only with an individual debtor who works for a living, and it's most appropriate to make this proposal in the beginning of the year. With some debtors, this refund can be quite a windfall, and if they haven't planned what to do with the money, this scheme can be a relatively painless way for them to pay back their debt.

Credit unions. This approach mainly works with the individual debtor who works in a company with a credit union or belongs to one through a trade organization. However, some credit unions now function much like banks, and almost anyone can go to them to take out a loan.

In either case, the credit union is often an easy source of credit to its members. Another benefit of using this source, you might tell the debtor, is that the loan can be used to consolidate all outstanding debts, including yours, and pay them off. Then the credit union can be paid off with one monthly amount (and this amount may constitute less of an immediate financial burden than the other debts).

Bank loans. The bank is another obvious source of a loan, particularly if a debtor has been with a bank for some time or has some collateral to put up for a loan. Again, the debtor can use this loan to consolidate other existing loans and pay these off.

Sometimes, a debtor may claim that it's impossible to get a loan because he or she already has one. In such a case, the debtor can probably refinance the original loan and pay you with the extra funds. For example, if the debtor has only a few months to go on the loan, he or she can ask the bank for more money and a loan extension.

Loan companies. If the debtor has a problem in getting a bank loan, there are always loan companies. The interest may be a little higher, but loan companies are usually willing to take a little more risk in return. As with the bank or credit union, the debtor can use the loan to pay you off, consolidate debts, and perhaps pay back even less per month.

Credit cards. Some debtors have a ready source of income with their credit cards. They simply have to ask for a cash advance on their MasterCard, Visa, or other account and can draw up to the limit of their credit. Then they can pay this off on a long-term basis by paying the minimum each month. (For example, with credit of $1,000, the minimum payment would be in the range of $25 per month.)

The credit limit on these accounts is usually   between $1,000 and $2,000, though some affluent debtors have built up credit lines of $5,000 (or even more) on preferred MasterCard and Visa accounts, or have special lines of credit they can draw on just by writing a check (such as a Chase Manhattan Advantage account, with a credit line of $5,000 or more).

Often debtors don't think of using their credit cards to get loans in order to make payments or consolidate debts. They just use the cards for making purchases. So suggest the possibility yourself.

Insurance policies. Some kinds of insurance policies (especially life insurance) can build up a cash value. If a debtor wants, he or she can cash it in or borrow against the policy at a low rate of interest.

Home or other property mortgage. This suggestion is most appropriate if the debtor owes you a substantial amount of money and owns some kind of property (for instance land, a home, an apartment, or an office building.)   In this case, the debtor may be paying off a mortgage, and if he or she has been making payments for some time, he or she might be able to refinance the mortgage to get a big enough loan to pay you off and perhaps take care of other debts.

Employers or business associates. Debtors often find their employers or business associates receptive to advancing them some money against a salary or other money they expect to receive. Some debtors may be very resistant to asking, since they don't want their employer or business associates to know about their financial problems. But when you've exhausted other alternatives, this approach might still be promising. Try to convince the debtor that the advance might help boost performance at work. You might say something like, "Well, wouldn't it be better to ask for some help at work? After all, if you don't have all these debts to worry about, you'll be a much more effective employee (or business associate)."

Or if you want to be a little tougher, you might suggest, "Well, I'm sure your employer (or business associates) will be understanding when you ask now. It'll be much better for you this way than if you wait for your creditors to take legal action, because they can go after your wages (or business assets), and then your employer (or business associates) will know anyway."

Friends or relatives. This is a good source of funds for debtors who have friends or relatives they are especially close to or who have money.

Again, many debtors resist using this source. Stress what they will be able to do with the money (i.e., "By borrowing, you can keep your high credit rating"). If they express concern about being able to pay back their relatives or friends, suggest that they can always borrow from another source, as long as they've got good credit.

Sale of household or office items or inventory. The sale of household or office items can be an excellent way to raise funds, and often it is quite a painless one. The debtor has probably accumulated many things not wanted or needed at home or business. In fact, such a sale may be more than a money-maker: it can unburden someone of unwanted items, or help a business run more effectively. (For example, a store can clear its shelves for newer and more salable stock; a wholesaler or manufacturer can get rid of excess office equipment or inventory.)

When you suggest such a sale, point out these advantages. Ask questions to find out what the person might most easily sell. For instance, you might say something like, "Is there some equipment you aren't using very much?"

Or, if you already know of such items, make a suggestion: "Why don't you put some photography equipment up for sale? You aren't using it anymore, and if you sell it now, you'll get more than if you wait."

Investors or new business partners. If the debtor has a business that has had problems, bringing in partners or investors could be another source of funds. Moreover, the additional capital could bring with it an infusion of much-needed management skills.

If the debtor is receptive to the idea of investors or partners, you might suggest some places to look (such as the business or money wanted sections of the newspapers.) The debtor could also put in an ad. Relatives and friends who might not agree to make a simple loan might be willing to extend an investment if they think the business has a hope of turning around and making money.

Helping the debtor find work. Another way to get your money is to help the debtor find work. If you have a position open, you could hire the debtor and provide compensation at the usual rate of pay. Then you either take it all and apply it to the debt (or perhaps just take 50% or so to give the debtor an incentive to keep working for you). If you set the wage scale, pay the debtor what you would anyone else. If the debtor has a business, you can pay his or her regular fee, or perhaps negotiate a slightly lower rate, given the situation.

If you have no work for the debtor yourself, suggest other job possibilities. The debtor might not be fully aware of his or her skills, and you could suggest additional job positions to consider. If you know of some temporary positions that would be easy to get, given the debtor's background and interests, suggest these. If you know someone who is looking for that kind of help, pass along the name.

Barter or trade. Engaging in barter or trade can work with some debtors, if they have something you want. If you can use the debtor's services, he or she can might be willing to work for you at his or her regular rates until you are paid. Or perhaps the debtor can offer some products in lieu of cash.

Another possibility is to take equipment or furniture, if the debtor is willing. Some may be, especially since this barter arrangement means they can immediately convert the item into a cash value rather than having to find a buyer and give the proceeds to you. If the debtor agrees to such an arrangement, work out a fair price for the item and bargain as if you were going to be buying the item for cash. The item might not be a priority one on your list; it could be something you might not normally buy, though you could use it if you did. If you have exhausted all other alternatives of getting paid for the moment, this might be the only way to receive compensation on the debt in the forseeable future.

Sources of Funds for Making Regular Payments

If the debtor can't pay you everything at once from one of these money sources, suggest sources from the list that follows to use for partial payments. Most of these sources apply to the individual with a personal debt, though in some cases they apply to the small businessperson, too.

If you do get the debtor to agree to use one of the following sources to make regular payments, be prepared to check up on the debtor if a payment doesn't come in on time. This way you can find out if the debtor is still getting income from that money source, suggest another source if that one has dried up, and remind the debtor of his or her obligation to you.

Payroll or unemployment check. If the debtor is regularly employed, ask for a commitment from his or her paycheck. If the debtor agrees to mail the payment to you, you might send a monthly reminder stating the remaining balance. If you see the person regularly, a friendly comment might be effective if you don't receive the payment when you should.

If the debtor loses a job or claims that his or her payment check isn't enough, ask about getting a payment from a spouse or children. Perhaps the debtor, spouse, or children are getting unemployment checks. You won't get much, but at least the payment is something (and it keeps the debtor in contact with you on a regular basis). If you aren't in touch for a long time, it's easy for the debt to grow stale.

Finding extra jobs. Another source of money is persuading the debtor to take on an extra job. If this is impossible, perhaps the debtor might ask a spouse or children to do the same.

If the debtor is receptive and needs help with job hunting, offer suggestions. You can refer to the previous section on helping the debtor find work.

Getting a bonus or salary increase. Some debtors might get more money or a promotion at work if they asked. Suggest the debtor try this, and perhaps even give some advice on how to get a raise. (You could suggest that the debtor might think about all the ways he or she has been valuable at work and has earned or saved the company money. Or he or she might offer to take on some extra responsibilities if needed.) And if the debtor is a freelancer, he or she could be encouraged to increase current rates if he or she can still maintain the same level of work or number of clients.

Getting extra vacation pay. If the debtor has a job where he or she can get paid for skipping a vacation, why not suggest this? Or suggest that a small businessperson or freelancer use a vacation to work.

Not all debtors may appreciate such a suggestion, particularly if they feel like a quick get-away to forget their bills. But some will be glad to have you suggest an approach they hadn't thought of before.

Additional income from rental properties. Some debtors might be in a situation where they could get extra rent. If the debtor owns some rental property and already has renters, perhaps he or she could raise the rent without any problems. Perhaps the debtor could rent out part of his or her home to a boarder temporarily. Possibly he or she has some unused office space to rent.

By asking questions, you can find out if a rental arrangement is a realistic possibility for the debtor. If it is, stress the benefits (other than paying you off) of such an arrangement. If the debtor rents out part of an office, for example, the renter may be able to help with the business by sharing secretarial services, answering phones, or even providing an expertise that could bring in new clients. A boarder in the home could provide a companion for the kids.

Turning hobbies into cash. A debtor with a hobby might be able to turn it into cash. Someone who collects things, for example, might advertise as an expert speaker on the topic. Someone who likes baking cookies might contact some a local grocery store to sell these products. Someone with a dog might offer a dog training service.

The possibilities are endless. What's more, if the debtor does develop a thriving business from a hobby, he or she will not only be able to pay you but will probably want to keep doing business with you, too.

Pensions. Pensions are another source of regular payment for the debtor who has retired. Some debtors may not feel comfortable dipping into this source of income. But if you suggest additional possibilities for the retired person, such as turning a hobby into cash, he or she may be more open to using part of a pension to pay you off.

Military reserve pay. Some debtors get a small stipend if they are in the reserves. They might be willing to contribute some of this.

Other Possibilities

As you can see, there are dozens of potential sources of income the debtor probably hasn't thought about. After you pose a few alternatives, encourage the debtor to start thinking. What ways does he or she currently earn money?   What other ways could income potential be expanded?

As you make suggestions, assume that the debtor really does want to pay you and is open to finding alternative sources of income to pay. Show you want to be helpful as you offer these suggestions, yet be firm about your desire to be paid. Let the debtor know you want to work together to find a solution and that some of your ideas for sources of money can help him or her in other ways besides paying you off. (For example, taking on a new job could give the person something very satisfying and fulfilling to do; finding work that pays more could lead to meeting new and interesting people.)

If, after all your attempts to be helpful, you find the debtor isn't responsive, that's an indication it's time to talk tough. Otherwise, do what you can to help the debtor pay.

CHAPTER 19:
Dealing with Disputes and Negotiating Settlements

If the debtor raises a real grievance when you appeal for payment, you normally have to resolve the dispute before you get paid. This involves some negotiation to work out a settlement.

There are two major types of grievances. In the first, the debtor doesn't agree with the amount due because of a mistake in the billing; in the second, the debtor has an objection to the product or service received, and as a result thinks he or she should pay less or nothing.

It's important to work out any grievance as soon as possible to speed up the payment process and increase your chance of keeping the debtor's good will. If you ignore the grievance, the debtor will probably continue to ignore the bill; then if you end up in court and the debtor defends the case, you will have to deal with the dispute.

Thus, as soon as the debtor gives a sign of holding back payment because of some grievance, acknowledge the grievance and deal with it. Although some debtors throw out a complaint as a red herring to stall or conceal an inability to pay, until you know or suspect this is probably so, treat any grievance as real. Even if you don't agree that the debtor has a valid grievance, treat it as real as long as the debtor feels a sense of injustice or is upset over whatever happened.

To settle the matter, you must show the debtor why he or she should pay all (or at least some of) the bill. Five key reasons to pay are outlined below.

(1) There is no real grievance--you have done nothing wrong.

(2) The grievance isn't as serious as the debtor thinks.

(3) In spite of the problem the debtor raises, you have done your best and have done everything you agreed to do.

(4) You will do everything you can to rectify the situation.

(5) Whether or not the grievance is valid, and no matter how serious or trivial it is, the debtor will benefit in continuing to work with you.

Your first step in working out the grievance is finding out about the debtor's view of the situation to determine if there is a real problem, how serious it is, what you or your company has done to create it, and what you can do, if anything, to solve it.

To get this information, let the debtor know you are concerned about finding out what happened and that you want to work with the debtor to resolve this situation. As soon as you hear the complaint, tell the debtor, "I'm glad you said that," to show you want to help. Then, if there are specific procedures to get the matter resolved (for example, the debtor should write the complaint in a letter and send it to a certain person), tell the debtor what to do. If you can handle the matter yourself, ask for the information you need or make a proposal on how you will deal with the complaint.

Sometimes you can work things out with a series of letters in which you refer to your records and any agreements you and the debtor made. Often, however, you will have to talk about the matter on the phone or perhaps arrange a personal meeting. Several calls or meetings may sometimes be necessary.

In any case, the process of resolving a dispute can go on for some time, although you should try to resolve it as soon and as favorably as you can. You might think of yourself as a negotiator trying to define a problem and work it out. Like any negotiator, you'll do best if you try to find a win-win solution where you and the other person both feel you are getting some benefit from the deal and feel good about the final resolution. If you come on too strong, thinking of the negotiation as an "I win/you lose" situation, the whole process will break down.

So consider the debtor's wants and needs as you go into the process. Listen to what he or she says; and assume, unless you have reason to believe otherwise, that he or she is sincere. Then use your common sense and judgment in cooperating with the debtor to work things out.

The rest of this chapter provides some guidelines you can use in working with the debtor and lists some responses to common situations that may come up. These are only some of the many possibilities, since there are so many possible disputes and ways to resolve them.

Some Guidelines for Discussing the Problem with the Debtor

When the debtor calls to complain or expresses a complaint when you call, there are certain procedures to follow in each conversation to increase your chances of coming to an agreement about the bill. In sequence, these include the following.

(1) Listen to what the debtor has to say without interrupting.

(2) Take notes on the debtor's position.

(3) Ask the debtor for more information, as necessary.

(4) Restate the debtor's point of view.

(5) State your own position or offer.

(6) Continue the process until you come to an agreement, or set up a time to discuss the issue again after you or the debtor get more information.

(7) Be firm yet flexible in changing your position or offer.

(8) Restate any new agreement clearly, get it in writing if you can, and follow up.

(9) If the debtor fails to keep the new agreement, consider the possibility that the debtor is using a grievance to delay. If so, get tough.

Listen to What the Debtor Has to Say Without Interrupting

When the debtor expresses a complaint, listen. The debtor may be angry, and may even yell or say obscene things, but just listen and let the person get the strong feelings and emotions out. Don't try to interrupt or yell back. If you do, you'll only make the debtor angrier and increase the level of conflict. Let the debtor ventilate and don't take it personally. Often the debtor is angry about the situation, not at you; even if you are the target, let the debtor get the feelings out. After the debtor has said what's on his or her mind, he or she will be ready to listen to you.

Take Notes on the Debtor's Position

As you listen to the debtor complain, take notes about his or her position. You can use phonetic shorthand or jot down key words, so you can easily recall what the debtor has said.

Ask the Debtor for More Information as Necessary

If you don't completely understand the grievance or the debtor has left out important details, ask for more information. Explain you need it because you want to help. Some things you may want to ask about are: What was the original agreement? When was it made? Who was supposed to carry it out? If the debtor wasn't satisfied at the time, why didn't he or she say something then? What kind of evidence does the debtor have about the problem (i.e., invoices, packing slips, letters about damages, etc.)?

Restate the Debtor's Point of View

Put the debtor's position in your own words in a calm, neutral way to show the debtor you understand what his or her position is, and ask the debtor to confirm that you understand it correctly.

> "Well, Mr. Jones, let me make sure I understand your complaint correctly. You say you went into the store to get the merchandise I sold you fixed, and the clerk behind the counter said, 'There's no problem. We'll take care of it.' Then, a few days after you got it back, it stopped working. So that's why you stopped the check. Is that right?"

Or, if the matter is a personal one, your comments might be something along the following lines.

> "Okay, Fred, let's see if we understand each other. You say the car you bought from me had some engine problems a few weeks after you bought it, and that's why you don't think you owe me anything: because you felt you should be able to deduct the repairs from the remaining balance. Is this correct?"

The advantage of making this restatement is that it ensures that you are both talking about the same thing; the debtor knows you understand. You have also defused the emotion from the situation by being calm. Finally, you have gotten the debtor to agree with you on at least some points. If you build on that yes to develop a series of yeses, you get the debtor in the habit of saying yes. He or she is then apt to be more positive when you advance your own proposal for settlement.

State Your Own Position or Offer

After listening to the debtor, you can state your own position or make an offer in light of the debtor's complaint. Depending on what the debtor has said, you may want to advance your original claim for payment again or make a counterproposal. But whichever you do, tell the debtor why it's to his or her benefit to pay you based on what he or she just said; otherwise you're back in square one. Consider something along the following lines.

> "Well, Mr. Jones, normally we would expect you to pay in full right now. But since the stereo isn't working, we feel it is our obligation to fix it or replace it. Since you did make the purchase and still have the equipment, you do owe us the money. But we will make sure you have the stereo you purchased in good working order within a week or we will give you a new one."

Another approach (for personal debts) might sound something like this.

> "Well, Fred, I understand your frustration when the engine conked out. But we did sign an agreement saying you were buying the car as is. I suggested that you take it to a local mechanic if you wanted to check it out before you bought it, but you drove it around a few times and said you didn't think it was necessary. So I feel I sold you that car fair and square--and you did drive it a few weeks before anything happened. So according to our agreement, which you signed, you still do owe me that money."

Continue the Process Until You Come to an Agreement or Set Up a Time When You'll Discuss the Issue Again

If the debtor turns down your offer, continue the process, and once again listen to the debtor and take notes, restate the debtor's position, and express your own point of view.

If the process bogs down, or if you need information that you or the debtor has in files elsewhere, suggest a break to gather this material. Then you can talk on the phone again or meet personally to hash things out. (For example, the debtor may need a copy of an agreement he or she signed, or you may need to send the debtor copies of recent repair bills to verify that you did the repairs in question.)

Be Firm Yet Flexible in Changing Your Position or Offer

As you continue to discuss the matter, show that you are firmly committed to getting the money you feel you are fairly due. Yet, if the debtor presents good arguments to support his or her case, be flexible and willing to change your position. If you can, imagine yourself in the role of an objective judge listening to the evidence on both sides, and ask yourself what a judge might decide. (After all, if you don't work something out, you might end up in this situation.)

Restate Any New Agreement Clearly, Get It in Writing If You Can, and Follow Up

If you can get the debtor to reaffirm the original agreement or make a new one, restate your understanding clearly and ask if the debtor agrees with it. Then tactfully suggest you would like to reaffirm this arrangement in writing so everything is clearly understood.

For example, you might offer to write up the new agreement. Then send it to the debtor for signature or arrange for the debtor to stop by to pick it up. If the debtor resists signing you can protect yourself to some extent by sending a confirming letter saying that this states what you and the debtor agreed to, and you will assume this accurately reflects the agreement unless you hear to the contrary. This letter is not as strong as a document with the debtor's signature, but it can be used if necessary to back up your position in court.

However you reach this new agreement, follow up afterward to be sure the agreement is kept. If you agree on a reduced amount due and the debtor has promised to resume sending in payments, write or call if any payment is missed.

If the Debtor Fails to Keep the New Agreement, Consider the Possibility that the Debtor is Using the Grievance to Delay

When you work out a new agreement in response to a complaint, the debtor will usually pay. In some cases a new grievance may arise, creating new payment problems (for example, you fix the debtor's stereo and set up a new payment plan, but the stereo breaks down again). If this happens, you have to settle the new grievance. However, it's also possible that the debtor is raising a new grievance to delay, or that he or she wasn't sincere in complaining in the first place.

If an agreement breaks down, be suspicious, and ask the debtor some hard questions. Why didn't he or she call you if there was a problem, rather than withholding payment? (For example, if the stereo broke down again, why wasn't it brought it in for a replacement?) Is some other problem causing the debtor to withhold payment (such as a financial problem)? Didn't the debtor agree to the new arrangement? If so, why didn't he or she keep this commitment?

If you think the debtor is trying to play games with you, you've got to get tough. You know you have exhausted your appeals in working with the debtor, and now it is time for the final demand. Tell the debtor you can't agree to any more delays; you have already been very patient; you have tried to work with the debtor fairly; and now you will have to take action (i.e., file a suit or take similarly serious steps).

Resolving Specific Complaints and Grievances

Depending on your business or credit arrangements, you are likely to hear certain types of complaints from debtors. Your own situation and policies will influence how you respond in settling disputes.

Generally, though, expect that you'll have to settle the grievance before you get paid. A third-party bill collector will try to get the debtor to pay the bill first and work out any problems with the creditor later, arguing, "You made an agreement to pay and it's not fair to expect the creditor to make any special arrangements with you until this bill is paid." But when you're still dealing with the debtor yourself, it may be difficult to make this kind of argument on your own behalf. You'll probably do better if you try to resolve the dispute first. If you can't get everything resolved in the same transaction, one possibility is to work out a staged arrangement, where you take some action to settle the problem and get some money, take a further action and get paid a little more, and so on until the matter is resolved. Then, too, be prepared that you might have to settle for a little less than the full amount to preserve good will and resolve the dispute.

In settling any dispute, first find out what the grievance involves, how serious it is, and why the person didn't tell you about it sooner. Note points of agreement; at a minimum you should be paid for the sum that is not in question. Then, when you feel you understand the problem, make a proposal about what you think would be a good way to resolve it. Be prepared for the debtor to disagree or come back with another proposal. In turn, you can reply with a counterproposal and arguments supporting your position. The process can go on for some time, depending on the complexity of the problem and how far apart you and the debtor are.

Whatever the situation, the key to finding a solution is remaining open and flexible so you come up with an arrangement that satisfies you while motivating the debtor to pay.

A good way to prepare yourself to deal with any issues that arise is to make up a list of common complaints and some ways to handle them. For convenience, list each complaint and the possible responses on a large index card. If you work with other people who handle complaints, suggest they make up a list of complaints and responses, too, and share your list with them. By having this list you will better know what to expect, say, and do, and thus will be better able to work out favorable agreements with your customers and clients.

Following are some common complaints and possible ways to handle them. Use them to get ideas that apply to you; then develop your own approaches.

You Overcharged Me for Merchandise or Services

An overcharge is a valid complaint, if true, but it's no excuse for ignoring your whole bill.

One strategy is to review the original agreement with the debtor by phone or in person to determine what prices, services, and merchandise were actually agreed to. During this discussion, determine whether there were any simple errors in computation or misunderstandings about the cost of the transaction or what was being offered. Then try to come to an understanding--possibly settle the matter with a compromise--and request full payment for the adjusted bill. Within a few days, follow up with a letter recapping your discussion and include an adjusted bill so there will be no further misunderstanding. If necessary, you can always use this letter and bill as evidence in court later.

Another approach, if it looks as if resolving the problem may take some time, is to ask the debtor to send you the amount not in dispute with the agreement that you will do some research on the disputed overcharges. Sometimes a debtor will resist this approach on the grounds that he or she wants to settle the matter completely before paying anything. This argument is often used as a way to stall. Legally, there is no reason a person should withhold payment on an undisputed amount. Debtors use this ploy to wear down the creditor and exact a settlement representing less than they owe.

Seek to convince the debtor to pay first. You could mention that the big credit card companies handle disputed debts this way, by collecting what's undisputed right up front from the cardholder while the rest is under discussion. Or you could appeal to the debtor's sense of fairness or interest in continuing to do business with you.

There's a Discrepancy in Your Billing and Our Records

This is a variation on the "you overcharged me" theme. If the discrepancy was in the debtor's favor, he or she would probably hope you didn't see it.

Debtors often use this discrepancy claim as a stall. One man who bought some books from me for resale gave me the excuse that he hadn't gotten around to paying my bill yet (it was now about 6 months overdue) because he had found a discrepancy in the number of books I said I gave him and the number of books he received. In addition, he claimed he couldn't find his own records at the moment because they were packed away in anticipation of a move. I should, I was told, wait until he could find them and correct the discrepancy. I eventually corrected the discrepancy for him in court.

Assuming for the moment, though, that the debtor is raising a legitimate concern, both you and the debtor should go back to your billing or shipping records and try to reconcile the discrepancy at this point. If you can't, one possibility (particularly if there isn't too much at stake) is to offer to split the discrepancy down the middle and ask the debtor to pay that. Failing that, you may have to base your case on who has better records.

As in the overcharge claim, work for a complete settlement and immediate payment. If it will take some time to resolve the discrepancy, urge the debtor to send you the undisputed amount. Then work on making an agreement about the difference.

There Were Some Damages or Shortages in the Product Received

Perhaps the debtor's claim of damages is true and some adjustments are in order. But this is no reason for the debtor to withhold payment for what was received in good condition. And if there was a problem, why weren't you advised you right away?

In some cases you may decide the debtor waited too long for you to make adjustments for damages or shortages. Then you will have to convince the person to pay the full amount regardless. ("You didn't tell us anything was wrong, so we already paid the shipper for the product.")

Other responses to damage or shortage claims might include offering to replace the damaged or missing merchandise or deducting the cost of the claimed items from the cost of the bill. However, if you consider any adjustments, do some investigating first, and try to involve the debtor in the process. Show that you want to work out a mutually fair and satisfying solution and that you hope the debtor will want to do so, too.

Some questions to ask in researching the situation include the following.

"What was damaged or missing? Who received this merchandise? When?" "What records do you have, if any, of what was received? Do these records show if anything was missing or damaged?" "Who is really at fault for the damage?"

Then, depending on what your research turns up, you can make any number of responses.

"If you would send us a copy of our original invoice, indicating the merchandise that was damaged or missing, we'll be glad to replace it. Please also include your payment for the amount due with this invoice." "We'll be glad to send you a replacement shipment for what was damaged or missing. We'll send it to you C.O.D. for the total amount of the bill." "Okay, go ahead and deduct the cost of the merchandise that's missing from the total bill."

However, avoid a response that commits you to sending additional merchandise and getting payment afterward. Don't say something like, "Sure. We'll go ahead and send you the merchandise you say was damaged or missing. Then, as soon as you receive it, please send us the full amount due." This helpful response doesn't make too much sense under the circumstances. The debtor has already delayed months paying the first bill. Why send anything else before getting paid?

The Merchandise Arrived Later Than You Promised; You Didn't Complete the Project in Time

At times a delay can mean the difference between whether a product or service is useful to the debtor and whether it is not; sometimes you have an airtight contract specifying delivery by a certain time. But other times a debtor can use a delay as a convenient excuse to evade payment.

Determine the real nature of the situation by asking the debtor relevant questions.

"Did an agreement state that the merchandise had to arrive by a certain time or that the service had to be completed by a certain date?" "Even if there was a delay, is the product or work still useful?" "Do you want to return the item in question? Why haven't you returned it already if there was a problem?" "Who was responsible for causing the delay?"

Depending on what your investigation turns up and what your own policies are, some possible responses will probably come to mind.

"If you want to return the merchandise, we'll be glad to credit you and deduct that from your bill. Your new total will therefore be _____. Can you send your payment for that amount now?" "It was only a few days late, and you can still use the merchandise. After all, all we said was that we would make every effort to ship it to you by that date. So the delay is no reason to withhold payment on your bill. Can you please send it at once?" "It took us a little longer than we expected to complete the work for you. Accordingly, we're willing to deduct the cost of the work we did for you after the tentative date we set for completion. However, we still expect payment for all the work completed before that time."

Your Product or Service Wasn't Satisfactory

Product or service satisfaction is another very subjective matter, one that raises many questions. By what standards is the debtor claiming the product or service wasn't satisfactory? What did the debtor expect? What did you provide? Why didn't the debtor express dissatisfaction right away? How serious was this dissatisfaction? Would someone else receiving the same product or service be satisfied? And what is a fair way of resolving this problem?

You and the debtor can end up engaging in lengthy, pointless debates when you discuss these and other issues related to the common complaint of dissatisfaction. In determining your position, decide how much you want to continue to do business with the debtor and consider how much the debtor is likely to want to continue to deal with you.

Start by asking some questions to find out why the debtor feels dissatisfied. Try to look at the matter from the debtor's point of view. Does the debtor really have some grounds for complaint, or is this a case of unjustifiable pickiness?

"What didn't you like about the product or service?" "What was the original agreement (if any)?" (For example, check if there was a written warranty attached to the product, or whether an implied warranty was involved. Ask what kind of service was promised. Find out if there is a contract stating exactly what would be provided.) "When did you feel dissatisfied, and why didn't you say something then?" "Would you like to return the item or get a replacement?   If so, why did you wait so long to say something?" "How much use did you get out of this product or service?" "Do you want to continue to do business together if this matter can be resolved satisfactorily?" "Were you satisfied with the products or services we previously provided?"

Imagine yourself as some outside arbiter or judge trying to get the facts of the case. What would the verdict be?

Then come up with a proposal, trying to be fair to both the debtor and yourself, based on the debtor's stated reasons for not paying, how strongly he or she feels, whether you or your company are at fault, and other relevant circumstances.

You might offer to replace or fix the product, if the debtor, in turn, pays you the full amount. Perhaps you could perform the original service again at your expense, assuming the debtor pays in full. You could deduct part of the bill to cover the costs of fixing the product or getting someone else to complete the project. You might send the debtor a copy of the contract to show that the debtor was expecting more than was stated in the contract, and that you did what was stated. Finally, you could decide to do some extra work for the debtor or ship some extra goods to compensate for the problems he or she has had if, in return, the debtor agrees to pay the original bill.

You or Someone Else Was Very Rude or Insulting to Me

Sometimes a debtor takes offense and won't pay because of the way you presented your bill or tried to collect. Or perhaps you did something after your bill arrived to anger the debtor, something that had nothing to do with the debt. Perhaps you argued with the debtor about something, or perhaps the debtor thinks you are responsible for doing something you didn't do.

All sorts of things can happen, and a debtor with financial problems may be especially eager to latch onto almost any incident as an excuse for not paying. Though such conflicts shouldn't have anything to do with the debtor paying a prior bill, often they do.

For example, I had some difficulty trying to collect from a struggling organization for goods I had sold. I received numerous promises that I would be paid; meanwhile the president came up with almost every excuse in the book to claim an offense and delay payment. When a book I had written was subject to a brief controversy (having nothing to do with the debtor), the president used that as an opportunity to delay communicating with me. There were a number of similar, and equally groundless, delays.

Although hard feelings shouldn't affect whether the bill is owed (unless, of course, you've used some damaging or harassing collection techniques that can subject you to a damage claim from the debtor), in practice you will usually need to clear up such feelings to collect the debt, unless you decide to get tough and go to court.

Get a discussion going on the problem and, as necessary, try to resolve any hurt feelings with apologies, explanations, or assurances that the problem won't happen again. At the same time, tactfully point out that the debt is still due, and that any problem since then shouldn't affect this prior obligation.

When you discuss the situation, begin with some questions to find out what occurred and why the debtor feels angry. Also ask what the debtor would like to do to feel better about the situation. "What happened? When did it occur?" "Who did (or didn't do) something?" "What can I (or my company) do to help solve the problem or make you feel better about this problem?"

Then, respond as appropriate, with an apology, explanation, or offer to make amends. "I'm sorry one of our people was rude to you. I'll talk to him and make sure it doesn't happen again." "I agree. I shouldn't have asked my secretary to call you about the debt, since it's a personal thing between us. But she takes care of all my correspondence, so she knows about these things. However, in the future, I'll contact you about it myself." "I'm sorry, we had a computer foul-up, and that's why the salesman didn't call on you when he was supposed to do so. But we've gotten our scheduling fixed up now. So I hope you'll accept my apologies, and we can work together without any problems in the future."

Finally, after the debtor's feelings appear to be soothed, diplomatically ask for your money. "Well, now that we have that resolved, will you need another statement, so you can take care of the account?" "I'm glad we've been able to take care of that problem. Now, if we can resolve one more thing, everything will run more smoothly in the future. If you can get your check in the mail in the next couple of days, we can close the books on this matter."

Coming Up with Your Own Solutions

The above complaints are only some of the common ones you'll encounter. You'll undoubtedly hear many other sorts of grievances and will have your own ways of resolving them.

So start brainstorming. List complaints, come up with questions to ask about them, and develop proposed solutions.

The debtor won't necessarily agree with all your suggestions (particularly since you're already involved in a dispute). But by thinking through likely problems and solutions, you can better direct and control the confrontation and end up with a solution that gets you paid.

CHAPTER 20:
Dealing with
Bad Checks

If you get a bad check despite your numerous precautions, handle it differently from past due accounts. You took the check instead of an immediate cash payment; you were not extending credit. Post-dated checks are a little different, since they are promissory notes to pay you at a certain time; even so, you took the check expecting the account still to be open with sufficient funds to cover your check.

Therefore, act much more quickly to resolve bad check problems, particularly if you believe fraudulent intent may be involved. You have criminal remedies, too, that can put pressure on the debtor to pay up.

There are three situations you're likely to encounter. First, there may be an error in the way the check was written. Second, the debtor may have unintentionally written a check on a closed account or on an account with insufficient funds. Finally, there is the possibility that the debtor intentionally wrote you a bad check.

When you receive the bank's notice with the bad check indicating what's wrong with it, you can determine the debtor's likely intentions from what you already know and from what happens as you communicate with the debtor about the check.

The question of intention can be a tricky one, and it should determine how you act. In some cases, for example, you may find that the debtor originally intended to write you a good check, but now, because of financial problems, either can't pay or decides not to repay you.

In any event, begin by assuming that the debtor made an unintentional mistake unless you have strong reason to believe otherwise. As long as the debtor's intentions seem sincere, proceed accordingly and treat the debtor with respect. But, once you start having doubts, get tough. You may have a criminal case if you act quickly enough. Although intentions are hard to prove, many states have stringent laws in this area.

The following sections describe how to deal with some common check-writing situations.

Checks With Errors

The most common errors that might slip by you are: the lack of a signature; discrepancies between the written and numerical amounts on the check (although if this is a small amount involving a matter of cents, the bank will often put it through for the lower amount): and the date of the check (checks dated more than three to six months earlier than the current date will commonly be considered undepositable by a bank).

Such errors tend to occur due to an oversight, and you almost certainly won't have any problem collecting. Simply send a letter or call the person to say you got the check back and would like another. When you get a new check, return the original one. Normally, that's all you have to do. To make it even more convenient for the person to send you another check, include a self-addressed envelope with your letter. For example, your first letter might go something like this (you'd say much the same thing on the phone).

> Dear _____:
> I just got your check for $50 back from the bank, because your signature isn't on it.
> Can you please send me another? I've enclosed a self-addressed envelope for your convenience--or you could just drop by with a new check in the next day or two, if you prefer. I'll return your original when I get your check.
> Sincerely,

When you do write or phone, don't sound as if you are blaming the person. For example, it's better to say you got the check back because "your signature isn't on it" than because "you forgot to sign it." The difference is slight, but if your words imply blame, you could antagonize the person about what was just an innocent mistake. It's also better to keep the original check until you get the replacement, in case there is a problem and you need the evidence to take to court.

When there is an error, the check writer will usually make out another right away. But be aware that some individuals and companies in financial straits may write a check with an error as a way to buy time. Even if you catch it before you send it through the bank, they have probably gained an extra week or two of credit by the time you discuss the check on the phone or by mail. If the check gets returned by the bank, they've gotten about a month.

If you do encounter delays in getting a new check, assume the person is stalling and get tough. Proceed now as if the debtor wrote you a bad check intentionally and you have to use pressure to collect. You won't be able to turn a check with an error into a criminal fraud case, as you might with a nonsufficient funds (NSF) check or one drawn on a closed account. But you can always use the check as evidence in court.

Unintentionally Bounced Checks

An occasional bounced check can happen to anyone, so unless you have reason to assume otherwise, respond as if the person has made a mistake. So proceed in a respectful, even friendly way, showing your good will and assuming the person will do the same.

Major Reasons for Bad Checks

These mistakes occur for a number of reasons.

The person may have been negligent in keeping track of the balance in the account, and may think there is enough money to cover your check when there isn't. (Unless the person has been grossly negligent, he or she can usually rectify the matter right away with another check. Otherwise, there might be some delay while he or she locates other funds to cover the check.)

On the other hand, the person may expect funds to arrive in time to deposit them to cover your check--but may not get the funds, or be able to deposit them in time. He or she may learn the funds take longer to clear than expected. (In this case you may be able to redeposit the check in a few days and have it clear; or there may still be problems.)

Another possibility: perhaps the person has the funds in the account, but encounters problems within the bank, which may have the money on hold as "uncollected funds" until the checks clear. Different banks have different policies on how long they place funds on hold, and delays are common, particularly on checks that aren't local. (This topic has been subject to much discussion and many calls for reform in recent years). The issue of what one can draw on in the bank, and when, can be genuinely confusing. Or the person might have a misunderstanding with the bank, in which the bank agrees not to put a hold on certain funds, but does. In any of these cases you can probably redeposit the check soon, once the funds are released; but problems are possible too. For example, if the person has had a series of checks bounce, he or she could have so many check charges, that the account becomes hopelessly out of balance. He or she might even close the account in frustration.

There are other possibilities, as well. The person may have closed the account to change banks and thought he or she left enough in the old account to cover outstanding checks--but didn't. It's even conceivable that the person wrote the check in the wrong checkbook by mistake, and then closed the account or didn't leave sufficient funds to cover your check.

Responding to Bounced Checks

If the bounced check is a first-time occurrence, a gentle reminder is generally sufficient to get the person to replace the check or let you know you can redeposit it immediately or in the next few days. Even if the situation has occurred before, it still may be a mistake, though such continuing problems suggest the person is negligent. So perhaps a more firmly worded reminder is appropriate.

In any case, act quickly. If possible, call or write the person the same day you get the check back. You want to correct the situation as soon as possible--or be in a better position to act if it appears that the person intentionally wrote a bad check.

If the check bounced because of insufficient funds or said "return to maker," request a new check or ask the person to advise you when to redeposit the check. If the person's bank is local (and therefore inexpensive to call), you might phone first to see if the funds are there to cover the check (just ask for the bookkeeping department, explain that the check bounced, and give the person's name and account number). Then contact the checkwriter to make sure he or she knows the check bounced and will be certain to have enough funds there to clear your check. On the other hand, if the check bounced because of a closed account, it's obvious that you'll need a new check.

If you want to add any charges for returned checks, advise the checkwriter accordingly. Some businesses normally add five to ten dollars to the original check (but if you add this much, be sure the debtor knows your policy in advance or you can create a lot of resentment). Another common approach is simply adding on your own bank's processing charge (usually only a few dollars). Some creditors don't add anything, in the interest of good will, since the debtor has already been charged by his own bank. In any case, I don't feel it's appropriate to come down too hard for an honest mistake. Certainly if the checkwriter is a friend or close business associate, you probably want to keep charges to a minimum. I find if I add just a few dollars to cover my costs or redeposit the original check without extra charges, in the long run this leads to a better relationship and more continued business.

Sometimes creditors will insist on getting the amount in cash, cashier's check, or a money order within the next few days and won't take replacement checks or wait for a redeposited check to clear, especially if they don't know the debtor well. But normally, if you think the checkwriter made an honest mistake, 't's appropriate to be understanding and assume the debtor's replacement or redeposited check will be good.

Whatever your policy on returned checks, when you first call or write, indicate that you think the situation probably occurred because of an oversight or innocent error. This way, the debtor doesn't feel you are accusing him or her of an intentional act.

An initial letter to deal with the matter might go something like this:

> Dear _____ :
> I'm sure this was an oversight on your part, but your check for $50 just came back from the bank marked insufficient funds.
> Can you please send me a new check immediately?   I will send you back your original. Or call me and advise me if I can redeposit the check.
> Sincerely,

Or perhaps try this more chatty approach used by one of my friends:

> Hi Marlene:
> Don't worry, it happens to us all sometimes, but your check for $50 just came back marked, "account closed."
> I'm sure there has been some mistake. Can you please send along a replacement check plus $3 for a total of $53 to cover check charges?   Then I'll send back your original.
> Sincerely,

Similarly, if you phone, keep it respectful and friendly. For example:

> "Hi, Charlie...Guess what?   I just got your check back from the bank. I'm sure it's all a mistake, so can you please send me another?   Or can I go ahead and redeposit this?"

> "Hello, Mr. Smith. There's been a problem with your bank, and we got your check back. I'm sure it's just an oversight, and I wanted to let you know, so you can send us another check. Or can you make sure there's enough money there so we can put it through again?"

In some cases the checkwriter may express concern about sending out a new check until you send back the original, fearing you may mistakenly cash the first check, too, and hoping to avoid the expense of stopping the check to prevent such a mistake. Normally you can assume this is a legitimate excuse, although some debtors who intentionally write bad checks use such requests as a ploy to get their original back.

Use your own judgment. If you want to hold the original until you get the new check, reassure the person that you won't cash both checks. If the person sounds sincere, you could agree to return the original, but make a copy of both sides before you do, in case you need this later for evidence. If the checkwriter lives or works near you, suggest you get together and swap checks. Alternatively, you could ask the person to send you a letter on his or her letterhead promising to send you a replacement check on receipt of the original check from you. Then, if necessary, you have documentation that the person is committed to replacing the check.

You're also in a stronger position if you can keep the person's check and return it after you and the checkwriter are squared away. But whatever you do, try to be diplomatic. If you encounter any resistance, you can always blame your adherence to procedure on your accountant.

Waiting for the Debtor's Response

After you have advised the checkwriter of the problem, guide your decision by the response.

In most cases, a person or company making an honest mistake will immediately act to make the check good and will tell you they are doing so. One auto company I called even thanked me for calling to inform them about the problem. They explained that they had transferred everything into a new account and written a check on the wrong bank; I was promised a new check in the mail that day. I got it two days later.

But sometimes, there's a delay. It may be legitimate, but watch out for a stall. And be careful that what starts as a real delay doesn't turn into a stall when the debtor runs into money problems.

The debtor may need a delay for several good reasons. He or she may have made a mistake in the account balance, and may need to get money into the account from another source. He or she may be waiting for funds to arrive or clear. Or he or she may have opened a new account, requiring some time for the funds to clear or for transferring funds into the account.

As long as the debtor indicates that he or she will make the check good right away or offers reasonable explanations about the delay, give the benefit of the doubt. Wait to see if the new check arrives or the expected funds are in the bank. If necessary, you can try to call the debtor's bank to verify that the promised funds are there.

In some cases a debtor may offer to make the bounced check good with a post-dated check or with a partial payment on account. Either alternative might be a good solution, though you're better off if you can press for full payment in the form of cash or a check or money order you can cash immediately.

An important reason for not taking a post-dated check or partial payment is that accepting either proposal changes the situation from getting a bad check, which may entitle you to certain penalties if you go to court to collect. If the amount is large enough, you may be dealing with a criminal matter. By contrast, if you accept a post-dated check, you are accepting a promissory note, which puts you in the position of formally granting credit. Accepting a partial payment also indicates your willingness to extend credit and eliminates any criminal remedies. Another consideration is that when you initially took the check, you weren't granting credit; if you have any alternatives, avoid doing this now.

However, if the debtor is encountering unexpected financial problems and you feel the person's original intentions were honorable, you may have little choice. In this case taking the post-dated check or partial payment may be the best thing to do.

In any case, after you and the debtor come to an agreement on resolving the situation, see that the debtor carries through. If the debtor doesn't make the check good as promised within a reasonable time (say a week or two) or if the post-dated check or partial payment bounces, it's time to be firm. And if you suspect fraud, act accordingly.

What to Do If You Suspect Poor Intent or Fraud

As soon as you feel the debtor isn't following through by sending you the replacement check, money order, or other promised payment, you should immediately warn the person that you intend to take action and then do it.

One good approach is to call or send a certified letter advising that you must receive payment by a certain date (a period of seven to ten days is usually appropriate) or you will take the action specified. If the money involved is substantial, or you know the debtor, visit him or her to find out what the problem is for yourself. Maybe this way you can leave with payment in full.

If you think the debtor is being lackadaisical about the matter, rather than deceptive, it is probably safe to accept another check, though to be doubly certain, call the debtor's bank first to see if it will clear. Alternatively, if you are now doubting the debtor's credibility and honesty, demand a certified check, money order, or cash.

Normally you should not tell the debtor's friends and associates about the matter, since you run the risk of being accused of defamation of character. (And remember, it is illegal for third-party bill collectors, including associates or employees of the creditor, to talk to others about the debt.) However, if you are a private individual trying to collect your own debt, you have a little more leeway in what you can do, since the laws relating to bill collecting in this area are interpreted more liberally. Also, the debtor is less likely to make claims about defamation when you are pursuing the matter yourself in a quiet, diplomatic way. For example, if you approach good friends of the debtor whom you know yourself under other circumstances, you may be able to gain their assistance in collecting your bill. But you have to approach them in a positive way. Point out that it's not that you want to come down hard on the debtor, but you'd like to get the matter settled without having to involve the courts or the police.

For example, a student named Bobby gave me a couple of bad checks for some merchandise. The first time this happened, I was able to reach him directly, and he came over the next day with some cash. When it happened again, Bobby was living with some friends without a phone. I spoke to a friend of his who also did some business with me and asked him to pass along my message, because I didn't want to have to call the police. A few hours later I got a call. Bobby was very apologetic, and was coming right over with my money. We continued to do business after that, but always in cash.

So as soon as you suspect poor intent or fraud, act to warn the debtor you plan to follow up quickly. If you wait too long, you eliminate a powerful remedy: the chance to file bad-check charges with the police. If a debtor knows you can and will do this after more civilized remedies have failed, he or she will realize that it would be wiser to pay. Furthermore, a debtor with poor intentions may know that by stalling you long enough your opportunity to file charges will pass.

I once got two bad checks from Marge, a client who gave me one check for consulting and another a few days later for one of my books. When I called, Marge said she and her husband would drive over with the money that night, and when I called to find out why they hadn't come, she said her husband hadn't gotten the money he expected to get from a friend. Instead, Marge said, she would send me a money order. Three days later, when I called to say it hadn't arrived, she said she would go to the post office to check it out. In subsequent calls, I got only friends or relatives, who passed on Marge's messages to me: she would call me back; the process of checking would take 30 days; she would send me a copy of the money order receipt; etc. Of course, the receipt never arrived, and attempts to get Marge on the phone continually failed. Strangely, Marge was always either out or expected home any moment.

Knowing what I know now, I would never have let this situation go on for so long. By the time I finally decided Marge no longer deserved the benefit of the doubt, it was too late. When I called the police, they told me that since the check was over 45 days old, they couldn't handle it. Now my only remedy was civil. Eventually I did collect by filing suit; but had I gotten tough sooner, I wouldn't have had to go to court.

How to Get Tough

You have a number of options to pursue when you get tough with a bad check writer, and you should mention the likely ones when you call or send your certified warning letter. This process is much like making the final demand in other debtor situations to be discussed later on in the book. You also have the options that may be available for collecting on a bad check: contacting the police and gaining extra damages.

You have four major options at your disposal.

(1) You can threaten to turn the matter to a collection agency or attorney.

(2) You can threaten to go to small claims court, either in the state where you got the check or where the debtor lives or does business. In some states, the law provides extra penalties for bad check writers. In California, for example, the legislature passed a law that entitles the creditor to seek triple damages in addition to the amount of the check and any regular check charges. If the creditor can show bad intent or if the debtor doesn't show up in court, the courts may award these damages.

(3) You can threaten to press charges with the police where you received the check. If you act before the time is up in that jurisdiction, the police will take a report on the matter: if the check is large enough, they will take an active role. Usually the larger the city, the higher the limits for handling bad checks.

Typically, though, if the police do take the case, they send out an officer to take the report and pick up the check. The case is referred to the sergeant in the fraud detail, who tries to contact the debtor and request that he or she pay you. If the debtor does pay (and the call by a police officer often provides sufficient incentive), that's the end of the case. Otherwise, if the police officer feels the debtor intentionally wrote a bad check (often hard to prove), the officer can send a report recommending charges to the D.A.'s office. Then it's up to the D.A. to file charges and prosecute the case, if he or she feels there's enough evidence. In other jurisdictions, especially smaller cities and towns, the police may be willing to take a report on a check that's older and for a smaller amount. However, that's all they may do: take the report.

Check with your local police to find out their procedures. Realize that in most cases the most the police can do is put some psychological pressure on the debtor by calling and asking him or her to pay. If the debt is an isolated incident or the debtor can explain why he or she intended to pay when writing the check, that's usually all the police will do. There has to be evidence of a bad intent from the start for any criminal case to hold up in court; most of the time that's so hard to prove that the police and D.A. won't pursue the case, and will claim the dispute is a civil matter.

Even so, with the average debtor, one who is basically honest, this pressure will work. For example, when I received a check for $550 that bounced, I wrote a warning letter after a month of delays saying that I would turn the matter over to the police if I didn't have the full amount paid to me in certified funds by the next day. When the man didn't respond, I went directly to the police. I knew I either had to either act now to do so or lose my police remedy forever, since it was the 44th day in a jurisdiction with a 45 day limit. The sergeant in the fraud division called the man who had written the check; he agreed to send me a certified check. I received it a few days later.

(4) You can threaten to file a complaint with the appropriate business organization, trade association or regulatory commission if the debtor is in business. A single complaint will probably not do very much by itself, but as soon as one of these organizations receives any complaint it opens a file. Then, if there appears to be a pattern of complaints, the organization will start an investigation, and that can lead to criminal charges.

This happened with that travel promoter, who wrote bad checks and failed to give refunds. After a half-dozen complaints had accumulated, the County D.A.'s Consumer Fraud Division assigned an investigator to the case. After about a month of looking into the case, the investigator turned the evidence over to the local D.A., who filed a number of charges. The promoter eventually ended up in jail for awhile.

Your get-tough letter or phone call should be short, to the point, businesslike, and firm. You don't want to come off emotional or angry; you simply want to show the debtor you really intend to do what you say. For example, your letter or phone call might go something like this:

Dear Mr. Andrews:

I still have not received the check for $250 you promised to replace the check I got back from your bank marked "account closed". I have tried to be patient in this matter, but it is now about five weeks since you gave me the original check.

This is my final request for payment in full for $250. A copy of the check that was returned to me is enclosed. I will look forward to receiving this payment within seven days or I will pursue other legal action. First of all, writing a bad check, if done intentionally, is illegal, and I will be reporting this check to the local police. Secondly, as you may or may not be aware, issuers of bad checks in our state are liable to triple damages as well as other penalties if the amount due is not paid and the matter goes to court. I hope it will not be necessary to take either of these actions, but I intend to do so if I do not receive your payment by June 15.

Sincerely,

Hi Frank . . . I'm calling since I still have not received the $250 which you promised to send to replace your check to me on a closed account. I've tried to be patient, but this has been going on for five weeks. So I wanted to call to make one last request before I take further action. I'll expect your payment within the next seven days, and then everything will be fine. Otherwise, I plan to report this to the local police and take the matter to court, where you may be liable for triple damages and other penalties. I sure don't want to do this, so can I count on your payment?

After you write or call, wait as long as you have said you would, and if the money doesn't arrive, act. You might make one last call to say you are on your way to an attorney, collection agency, police station, or the courts to file, and see if this rouses the debtor to act right away. But at this point you've done what you could, and you should consider the matter a lost cause. So do whatever you said you would.

Then if the debtor contacts you and wants to settle, as the client who gave me two bad checks did, add on any extra costs incurred in taking these actions (such as your costs for filing or serving papers) and other charges if you feel in a strong position. For instance, if your courts offer triple damages, you might add on a little extra for penalties, though not so much that the debtor refuses and you have to go to court.

If you have to pursue a bad check matter past the letter-writing and phoning process, you are justified in getting tough and negotiating with the debtor to settle from this position of toughness. After all, if you have to take the matter further to get the debtor to respond, you're entitled to more, and in a bad check case, you've got an important edge, because bad check writing is illegal. So you probably have an open and shut case in court, and possibly grounds for a criminal complaint, too.

CHAPTER 21:
Making the
Final Demand

Normally you can settle with people who owe you money through reminders, appeals, or discussion.

But then there are the hard core collection problems: people who continue to claim they have no money and aren't interested in settling a dispute, or are using it as an excuse not to pay. Such people want to do all they can so they don't have to pay, whether they owe the money or not.

Once you have given up on reminders and firm yet friendly appeals, it's time to switch gears and move on to the final demand.

You have to assume the debtor cannot or will not pay the bill, though you still want to persuade him or her to do so. Since these other appeals haven't worked, your recourse now is to the most basic, intense appeal: the appeal to anxiety or fear. But be careful not to be too heavy-handed. You may want your communications with the debtor to sound threatening at this point, but you don't want to threaten anything illegal. Doing so may result in a charge of extortion.

Arriving at the Final Demand Stage

Some creditors arrive at this stage much sooner than others: only a few reminders and appeals and that's it. Others let the process drag on much longer, giving the debtor the benefit of the doubt.

However long it takes, the final demand stage occurs when you have given up on trying to be friendly and understanding and want to give the debtor a last chance to pay you before you take some further serious action, such as turning the account over for collections, going to a lawyer, or filing in small claims court.

If the account is small enough (say under $50) you may want to write it off if the debtor doesn't respond to this last demand, since it will probably cost more to collect than it's worth. Even so, make your last demand convey a feeling of urgency, a sense that the debtor had better act now or suffer the consequences.

No Going Back

Once you make your final demand, there is no going back unless the debtor makes you a counter-offer. If you make a demand and retreat from it to try reminders or appeals again, you look ridiculous.

When you make your demand, be aware that you have alternatives if the debtor doesn't pay in full. You can: hire an attorney; turn the matter over to a collection agency; go to small claims court; or work out a settlement or extended payment plan with the debtor, if the debtor contacts you. Of course, you also have the option of writing the debt off and chalking it up to experience.

Types of Demands

Although I prefer a single "this is your last chance" letter or phone call (since you already have been in touch with the debtor numerous times) some creditors use a series of letters or calls. Each one gets a little tougher, but only the last sets the date when the debtor must settle up or else.

In either case, your letter or call will typically contain these elements:

(1) A serious tone, stressing the urgency that the debtor act now before you take action.

(2) A brief statement of the problem(s) you face because of the uncollected debt. In some cases creditors write up a brief objective overview for the debtor and have a summary document they can use if the case goes to court.

(3) A proposal to take further action that will have negative effects on the debtor. Creditors often temper this by saying they regret having to take this action, but feel they have no choice because of the debtor's lack of response.

(4) An offer that the debtor can avoid this action by paying you or contacting you now to discuss the matter.

(5) A date when you plan to take any action if this is expected to be your last communication. Otherwise just talk about the coming action. Once you state a date, you're committed and there's no going back.

Making a Preliminary Demand

If you have decided to use one or two demand letters or calls before the final one, your tone should still be urgent and demanding. However, you should talk about taking further action if the debtor doesn't respond rather than stating specifically when you plan to take it. Emphasize the losses to the debtor if you have to take this action.

Some Preliminary Demand Letters

A few examples of representative preliminary demand letters follow. All of them can readily be turned into final demands by adding a statement about when you plan to take action and what you will do. Following is an example.

Dear Mr. Martin:

You have not answered the many notices we have sent you about your past due account of $845. By not responding, you are forcing us to consider further steps. We value your business, and we hope that you value us as a vendor. We do not wish to lose you as a customer. We hope that you don't force us to take further steps to collect this debt. However, we will have to take additional steps to collect this overdue balance if it is not paid within ten days of this letter's date.

Please--pay the overdue balance immediately.

Very truly yours,

Note that the demand still involves an appeal, but that this time the appeal is to fear and anxiety. The letter emphasizes that the debtor will experience a loss of good will, and there is a threat of other action. But the specific action is left vague.

Other preliminary demand letters may explain in more detail about the past problem, noting that the creditor has tried hard to settle the situation but the debtor hasn't responded, leaving the creditor little choice.

Here's another sample letter, explaining that the creditor has tried to settle the matter in the past, and is now making one last request.

Dear _____:

We do not like to write this kind of letter. But you give us no choice.

We have asked you repeatedly to pay your past due balance of $750. You have yet to respond, despite our many attempts to remind you.

So we must now turn your account over to our attorney for collection. We do not want to do this, because we have done business together for a long time.

A lawsuit will not only be expensive for you, but also time-consuming.

Because of our long business relationship, we will allow you one last chance to pay this bill. Please send your payment today. Thank you.

Sincerely,

At this final demand stage, it's usually more appropriate to send a letter--and it's helpful to have a copy you can use to describe and support your case if you go to court. But if you have known the debtor for some time, a personal phone call with the same serious, urgent tone might be in order. Your letter or call might sound something like this:

> Hello Jim . . . You know, I'm really disappointed that you've been ignoring my many requests to settle your debt. We've talked about this so many times, and I've made every attempt to work with you. But the money is still overdue. I'm beginning to feel that the only way to resolve this is to take further legal action, though I would prefer not to, since we've known each other so long. So I thought I'd get in touch with you one more time and give you another chance to settle the matter. Can you send in your check today?   Let's get this resolved so I don't have to turn the amount over for collection.

The Short Collection Message or Memo

Another possibility is the short collection message or memo, which states how much is due and urges the debtor to contact you quickly before you take further action. You can write up these messages yourself or obtain preprinted ones at a stationery store. A short message designed to be a first demand might sound something like the following.

> Dear Mr. Ryan:
> We must receive your entire overdue balance of $625 within ten days or we will pursue serious collection measures.
> Sincerely,

> Dear Mr. Ryan:
> If we do not receive payment immediately on your long-overdue balance, we will institute more serious collection measures. We have requested payment repeatedly and have received no response. We cannot wait any longer.
> Sincerely,

If you wish, include a reply form to make it easy for the debtor to respond, or include space for the debtor to note a reply on your letter. A typical reply section might look like the checklist below.

_____ I am enclosing payment

_____ I made payment on _____

_____ My check number was _____

Additional comments:

The Telegram or Mailgram

Still another type of preliminary demand is the brief telegram or mailgram to make the debtor pay more attention. It's like the final demand telegram or mailgram, except you don't set a date on which you will act. Below are some examples.

> WE MUST RECEIVE YOUR OVERDUE BALANCE OF $675 PROMPTLY OR YOU WILL BE REFERRED TO OUR ATTORNEY. PLEASE SEND YOUR PAYMENT TODAY.

> UNLESS YOU CALL US IMMEDIATELY CONCERNING YOUR LONG PAST DUE BALANCE OF $175, WE WILL REFER YOUR ACCOUNT TO A COLLECTION AGENCY.

How Long to Wait

After you send out your preliminary demand, wait. (Two weeks is probably as long as you should delay.) Then follow up either with one last, even more sharply worded preliminary demand, or, as I prefer to do, go immediately into your final pitch. The matter is looking more and more hopeless, so why wait?

Making a Final Demand

Whether you have attempted a preliminary demand or not, you have given up on appealing to the debtor. Now it's time for your last demand to let the debtor know this is it!

Tell the debtor he or she has exactly X number of days (five is recommended, but you can go up to ten days at the most) to get payment to you or you will take the promised action. This time, specify what you plan to do.

Make this last push in writing, even if you know the debtor. It's a good idea to send this communication via certified mail. This will give the debtor even more indication that you're serious, and it's proof, if you need it in court, that the debtor has received your letter and knows you have demanded the debt.

Depending on circumstances, there are four types of final demand letters.

(1) The complete letter detailing the situation and your frustrations over your inability to collect. This is appropriate if you haven't stated the information in a preliminary demand.

(2) The referral letter, if someone else in your company has been dealing with the debtor and you are now taking over the matter for this final push.

(3) A brief letter demanding payment.

(4) A telegram or mailgram demanding payment.

The Complete Letter

Essentially, you explain the situation as if you were making a preliminary demand. But you sound even tougher at the end by stating the kind of action you plan to take if payment isn't received or the matter satisfactorily disposed of by a certain date.

Here's how it might look.

> Dear Mr. Hayden:
>
> Your account of $250 is still overdue after 6 months, despite my extending you every courtesy in trying to settle the matter. You have acknowledged the debt and agreed to send the money, but then, over and over again, no check.
>
> I can't wait any longer, and much as I don't like to do this, I will be filing suit in small claims court on the afternoon of September 5 if I don't receive your payment in full by then.
>
> As you may be aware, your costs can increase considerably if I am forced to do this, since once a judgment is rendered against you you become liable for court costs and additional interest and collection expenses. I hope I will not have to take this action, but if I don't have your payment by noon on September 5, this is what I intend to do.
>
> Sincerely,

Note that the debtor still has an out: by paying. If appropriate, you can give the debtor an option of working out extended payments or some other settlement with you. But he or she must respond, or you take the action you threaten.

The Referral Letter

Use this type of final demand if an associate, assistant, or separate department in your company has been in touch with the debtor. The advantage of sending this kind of letter after someone else has dealt with the debtor is that it shows you consider the matter serious enough to give it extra personal attention.

It might look something like this.

Dear _____ :

Your overdue account for $250 has just been referred to me, marked "final action."

Since we like to give our clients every courtesy and extend the benefit of the doubt if there's a problem, I am sending you this letter as a last resort.

Because you have not responded to previous requests, this is our last communication to you. Will you please send me your check for $250 or call me personally so we can work out some mutually satisfactory arrangement to settle this debt?

I will hold your account for 10 days, until December 10, in the hope we can resolve this matter amicably. If not, I will have no alternative but to turn your account over to our attorney for collection.

I hope it will not be necessary to do this, because, as you know, an assignment for collection can seriously damage your credit reputation.

Sincerely,

The Brief Letter

This letter assumes the debtor is well aware of the situation and merely needs to know you have lost patience and will take a specified action if you aren't paid by a certain date.

Three examples follow.

Dear _____ :

If your check for $250 is not in this office by September 15, we will refer your account to a collection agency.

Sincerely,

Dear _____ :

Your long overdue balance is for $250.

We have held up legal proceedings to avoid the added costs of a court action. This letter is to advise you that we can wait no longer and will take legal action for payment in full, unless payment is received within 7 days from the date of this letter.

This is our last request. You will receive no further notices from us about this matter.

Sincerely,

Dear _____:
WE CAN'T WAIT ANY LONGER.

We're tried to be patient and reasonable about the $250 you owe us, but you have ignored all our requests.

Thus, if you don't send your check to us by September 15, WE'LL HAVE TO TAKE MORE DRASTIC ACTION AND REFER YOUR ACCOUNT TO COLLECTIONS.

Sincerely,

The Final Telegram or Mailgram

This can take the form of a "Final Request" memo or an actual telegram or mailgram advising the debtor to act to stop immediate action.

For example, a sample final request form might begin with a head-line and then state the essentials briefly.

FINAL REQUEST

This is our final request for payment on your past due account. We have tried to work out the problem with you. But you have not even had the courtesy to reply to our past letters.

As you know, your credit is very valuable to you, and you can damage your credit, as well as incur substantial costs in time and money when your account is placed for collection.

But you can prevent this by sending us your check for the full amount--$250--or calling us to settle this matter.

We will wait until December 15, and then assign your account to a collection agency.

Sincerely,

If you send a telegram or mailgram, a few lines will do.

THIS IS A FINAL NOTICE. YOUR ACCOUNT OF $500 IS BEING REFERRED TO AN OUTSIDE COLLECTION AGENCY UNLESS WE RECEIVE YOUR PAYMENT BY SEPTEMBER 15. SEND IT TODAY.

Waiting for the Debtor's Response

After you send out your final demand, it's up to the debtor. Don't get impatient and call to find out if the debtor received your letter or ask about his or her reaction. Your call will only defuse the urgency of your letter.

Just wait. Your last pitch may bring in some money. But often, when a debt problem has gotten this far, a final demand is largely a formality to show the courts you have formally demanded your money and gotten no response.

If the debtor does finally pay at this point and appeals to you to do further business together or preserve a friendship, that's up to you. But ask yourself whether, if you've had so much difficulty collecting this time, you want to keep the door open for further problems. Has the debtor satisfied you sufficiently that it won't happen again?

In any event, if you decide to give the debtor another chance, I would recommend being firm. Tell the debtor you will not let the problem go on for so long next time. Take extra steps to protect yourself in advance, such as telling the debtor that from now on everything is cash or C.O.D. until the debtor has proved his or her good faith to you again.

If the debtor doesn't respond, do exactly what you said: refer the debt to a lawyer or collection agency, go to court yourself, or if it's not worth it, write it off.

The following section of the book describes the next stage of the process: assigning a debt for collections or going to court.

CHAPTER 22:
How and When
to Get Tough

At some point, you will decide that dealing with the debtor your-self isn't working, and that you need outside assistance to stand any chance of getting your money.

This decision may occur at different times during the reminder-appeals-demand process for different people, because situations and debtors vary so widely. Some people or companies prefer to crack down sooner, while others want to give the debtor a longer grace period to maintain good will. The size of the debt and the financial condition of the debtor make a difference, too. Is the debtor able to pay, but refusing to acknowledge a legitimate debt? Has the debtor simply encountered hard times--and if so, how likely is he or she to come into some money? Is a bankruptcy likely soon?

This chapter describes the factors to consider in deciding when to get tough and your major options.

When to Get Tough

Getting tough comes at the end of a process that usually leaves the creditor with feelings of frustration, hostility, or anger. He or she is often frustrated by an inability to motivate the debtor to pay, despite repeated attempts, and annoyed or resentful the debtor hasn't paid what the creditor considers a rightful debt.

The option to get tough exists at any time during the process, since a creditor can always go direct from reminders, appeals, or a final demand to one of the options described here. For instance, some cred-itors short circuit the appeals stage to take immediate strong action, if they sense the debtor is likely to skip town or that his or her business is about to go bust.

The following factors will help you decide when to make the move yourself. Consider them along with your own personal style, and do what feels comfortable for you.

Size of the Debt. If you're trying to collect a big debt, you'll reduce your risks of losing big if you move faster and more aggressively than with a small debt.

The Age of the Debt and Common Payment Patterns. How old is the debt? Is it owed to you by an individual or a business? What is the payment agreement? If the debt is with an individual client or customer, you will probably want to step up the pressure sooner (say after 60 or 75 days); individuals are usually expected to pay upon billing. What's more, a single person can easily move and disappear. On the other hand, if the debt is with a stable, solid business, the debt collection process can be drawn out longer, since the business may simply have a relatively slow pay cycle. If you wait a few months before getting tough, the business will still be around. Remember that when you deal with a business, there can be many extenuating circumstances that can slow things down, like seasonal or temporary slumps, changes in management, and problems with record-keeping.

The Debtor's Situation. Ask yourself these questions to assess the situation: Is the debtor solvent or teetering on the verge of bankruptcy? Is any financial problem temporary or seasonal, or is it apt to continue? Is the debtor likely to receive a substantial amount of money soon, and, if so, how certain is this?

The Possibility of Bankruptcy. If there is a possibility of bankruptcy with a business, you should probably move in quickly. If you can do so three months or more before the bankruptcy petition is filed, (in other words, secure your assets and possibly make an early partial settlement or affirm your debt with a judgment), you will be at an advantage. Remember, the entire business gets liquidated in a bankruptcy, and you will almost certainly be competing with other creditors for the assets that remain. When dealing with an individual, however, you may want to wait things out if pressure from you may force a bankruptcy. A bankrupt person has about $8,000 in exemptions, and there may be little or nothing left for creditors.

The Power and Status of the Debtor. This factor can work both ways. For example, a high-status powerful debtor who is especially concerned about reputation may ignore routine requests. But once you get serious, he or she may respond, fearing your actions may leave the blot of a judgment or negative credit report on his or her record. On the other hand, if the debtor is powerful in your community or industry, there may be negative fallout if the debtor decides to become vindictive and spreads disparaging comments (true or not) about you. You might find yourself losing friends, or perhaps your own business might even decline.

Your Relationship with the Debtor. Is the debtor a stranger? A business associate? Someone you know personally? How much do you value keeping the debtor's good will? Once you get tough, you are likely to break up your relationship permanently. Give this matter due consideration. Then, once you decide to act, stay the course.

The Attitude of the Debtor. Do you feel the debtor sincerely acknowledges the debt and is simply having trouble paying due to financial constraints? Is there a dispute to work out? Or does the debtor seem to be stalling and giving excuses just to buy time? If you suspect deceit at this stage, it may be time to crack down.

Your Own Financial Situation. Another issue may be how long you can carry the debt. The stronger your financial position or the larger your company, the better off you're likely to be. Alternatively, if you are an individual with an average income or have a small business, you may not be able to continue the process as long.

Your Time Constraints and Preferences. Going after hardcore debtors can become wearing. After a point, it may make more financial sense to turn the matter over to someone else rather than continuing to invest your energy (or that of others in your company) in trying to collect. After all, if you can make more money pursuing your own business, why play bill collector?

Your Attitude toward the Debtor. Besides your attitude toward debtors in general, you may have feelings about a particular debtor that incline you either to continue on a relatively lenient course or to start getting tough. You may genuinely like one debtor, and want to maintain the relationship even though he or she owes you money and makes one excuse after another for not paying. In another case, you may consider the debtor a jerk or a deadbeat, and get angry during every discussion with the person. In this case, you probably won't care if you ever do any business (or even talk to each other) again.

Besides the major factors just described, other elements may be important to you. There are no absolute rules in deciding when to get tough, only guidelines for choosing what's best for you. Everyone has a personal style; some people prefer to give others many chances and promote good will; others think more about the bottom line and like to act more firmly, quickly, and decisively from the start.

Weigh the factors that seem relevant to you in setting your general guidelines and deciding how to act in a particular case. Then act to express your personal style.

Your Four Options

Once you decide you can no longer handle collecting a debt yourself, you have to determine which option would be best for you. The option you select will depend on the type of case, size of debt, type of debtor, and debtor's likely response. You may also want to use a combination of options, though you should only use them in sequence, one at a time.

This section describes each option briefly and the major reasons for choosing that approach. The four types of options, previously mentioned, are: the pre-collection letter; the attorney; the collection agency; and small claims (and sometimes municipal or superior) court on your own.

The Pre-Collection Letter

The pre-collection letter approach involves sending out a series of letters of increasing intensity asking for the money and threatening legal action if the money isn't paid. This is probably similar to what you have already done. However, the difference is that these letters come from someone else, so the debtor takes them more seriously. He or she can see that you have taken another step in collecting your money and may go further if you do not receive payment soon.

There are two types of pre-collection letter services. One type, offered by independent companies, simply provides you with a series of two to three letters and send them out for you at specified intervals (usually every 7-10 days) until the complete letter series has been sent--or until you have advised the company not to send out any more letters because you have gotten your money. Normally, you have to buy a minimum number of letter series to different debtors (generally 25 or more) to sign up with this service. The price is about $7-9 per debtor; you pay no commission, and keep the full amount of any payments, which are mailed directly from the debtor to you. However, since you will have to make a commitment for a minimum number of letters, you should probably figure your initial investment at around $200 to get started with one of these services.

The other type of pre-collection program is offered through a collection agency (organizations about which we'll learn more later), and is sometimes called a free demand service. The agency sends out one or two letters, much like the independent company does, charges about $8 for the service, and directs the debtor to send the full amount to you. The difference is that if the debtor doesn't respond within a specified time limit (typically 10 days from the final notice), the collection agency transfers the debtor into hardcore status, and then collects for you using its usual collection procedures and contract arrangements. Again, you may have to agree to a minimum commitment of letter sets (whether or not you actually need to use them all right away), although the agency usually asks for fewer--commonly about ten--than a service that only sends letters. This is because the agency will get additional business from you if the letters don't work. Going the agency pre-collection route, your investment will be about $80 for the letter, and perhaps a small agency set-up fee of $40-50 to put you on the system.

Using this kind of pre-collection service makes the most sense when you have two specific types of collection problems.

(1) A number of small debts, including bad checks, where it is not worth the effort to make a lot of follow-up phone calls yourself. (A cer-

tain percentage of these debtors will pay up if they get these letters.)

(2) A debt that has dragged on with a normally solid, reputable individual or company, and the main problem is slow payment. This individual or company will probably pay you eventually, but may need more prodding than you can give. At the first whiff of trouble brewing (trouble that might result in a damaged credit reputation), this debtor will likely pay. An outside collection letter is often all this individual or company needs to be motivated to write that check.

By contrast, if the debt is big, or if the debtor has financial problems or is trying to get out of paying, you won't want to use this kind of service. It will only prolong the process. Moreover, a savvy debtor will not be impressed, having received similar letters before. He or she will simply let the letters run their course, and count on having an extra 30 to 60 days before having to deal with the debt in a serious way.

The Attorney

An attorney packs more clout than collection letters do. After a letter or two, he or she can take the case directly to court, whereas the former method only warns about turning over the matter for legal action. An attorney's letter may get more attention from many debtors who are afraid of being hauled into court and assume such a letter means the attorney is getting ready to file suit.

However, unless the debt is large, it doesn't make sense to hire an attorney. If the amount is below, say, the $1,000 to 1,500 range, you can usually forget about this alternative. You can handle the matter more quickly and economically in small claims court by yourself. Even if the debt is a little higher than the small claims ceiling, forcing you to shave the claim somewhat, you'll still come out ahead (assuming you win) compared to working with an attorney.

An attorney usually won't touch a case on consignment if it's worth less than $2,000 (and then only if he or she thinks it's an easy win). On the other hand, if the lawyer agrees to take your case on a fee basis, you still have no guarantees you'll collect on a judgment in your favor, but you'll have additional lawyer fees to pay. You can figure on paying between $75-150 per hour, plus out of pocket expenses for filing fees and court costs. Your court costs will be added on to your judgment if you win, but you probably won't get lawyer's fees unless your agreement with the debtor specifies this.

There's one possible exception. If the lawyer will make a few calls or write a letter or two for you for a small charge, an attorney may be able to help you collect a relatively small debt. For example, a recently graduated attorney just starting a practice might be an ideal candidate to write such a letter on his or her letterhead, since he or she is eager for business and won't charge much. Since the debtor won't know that the lawyer isn't planning to follow through (or how experienced he or she is) it doesn't matter what attorney you use. All that's necessary is a letter that's "lawyerly" in appearance and composition on good stationery. Your cost might be about $25-50.

A variation: some lawyers might be willing to make a phone call or write a letter or two for a percentage if you collect anything within 10-15 days after the letter. One attorney agreed to do this for me for 15% of whatever he collected. This came to a fee of $75 on a $500 case.

However, while lawyers can be of limited use for small accounts, you are almost always better off letting a collection agency or letter service send out your letters in these cases. In fact, some collection agencies affiliated with lawyers can send out a letter under their attorney's name, and if they send it as part of a pre-collection package, it will only cost you about $8 for the letters, versus $25 or more if you go to an attorney.

By contrast, when your debt is substantial--say, $5,000 or more-- and isn't likely to be settled by mediation (which is where agencies are good), I would go right to an attorney. You'll get much speedier action. After a letter or phone call or two, the attorney can take the debtor right to court. If there's any chance of the debtor getting rid of or hiding assets, a good lawyer can initiate attachment proceedings to prevent your assets from disappearing.

The Collection Agency

The collection agency will use some of the same strategies you have: letters and phone calls appealing to the debtor. But a key difference is that the agency is a third party, so the debtor takes the contact more seriously. What's more, agency collectors are usually trained pros who have learned the most effective phone techniques to get payment.

Collectors can make some appeals you can't. Because you are directly involved in the case, the debtor may have some feelings of hostility or resentment toward you that are getting in the way of paying. However, a third party caller may be able to persuade the debtor to put such feelings aside, to acknowledge the debt, and to recognize the possible consequences of failing to pay.

Another advantage of collection agencies is that they are normally more systematic than you at following up on an account. This is, after all, their business. Even if you haven't been able to mediate a dispute yourself, collection people may be able to. If there is a dispute, they can often get payment for the non-disputed amount while a conflict is being settled, whereas when dealing with you a debtor may want to resolve all disagreements first.

An agency can also be helpful if you have problems locating a debtor; the debtor-tracking services agencies offer are known as "skip tracing" in the trade. In addition, a collection agency's access to credit information through reporting bureaus can help determine the debtor's real financial situation. And some agencies can report your problems with the debtor to the credit bureaus. This can be a powerful tool in winning payment from debtors who fear a bad credit report.

Most collection agencies won't charge you unless they collect; they tend to work on a commission basis. As one agency describes its services, "If there's no collection, there's no fee." Typically, agency fees range from about 20% for large volume commercial accounts to 50% for most individual assignments. The agency determines its fee based on a number of factors, including the size of the debt, its age, how collectible the agency considers it, and the number of accounts you are assigning.

As noted earlier, many agencies also offer a pre-collection or free demand service, whereby they send out one or two letters advising the debtor that the account will be assigned to a collection agency, or that further, more drastic collection activities will occur unless payment is made. Then, if the creditor doesn't receive payment by a certain date, the agency gives the account its usual treatment.

Using a collection agency is most appropriate under the circumstances listed below.

(1) You have small debts from consumers, clients, or business deals that are too small for an attorney, and you don't want to take them to small claims court yourself.

(2) You have a debt that can probably be settled if you work out a dispute with the debtor, but you are unable to resolve it yourself. Note that, while you have the option of going to court, it may be better to use a collection agency first if: (a) you have no time or interest in going to court yourself; or (b) the dispute is complex enough for you to stand a chance of losing your case. (Even if the case is large enough for an attorney, it may be better to let a collection agency mediate it: unlike attorneys--who are trained in an adversarial setting--collectors are usually trained to work with the debtor to resolve the problem.)

You may feel you need an attorney eventually for a large debt, but don't know a good collection lawyer. In this case, advise the agency that you think legal action will probably be necessary to be sure you choose an agency willing to aggressively pursue legal means, if needed. Such an agency will probably work with a lawyer who specializes in collections, and may be able to provide a referral.

Going to Small Claims, Municipal, or Superior Court Yourself

If the amount of money owed to you is small and you want to try for the total due yourself, your best option is small claims court. Rules differ from state to state, but generally you can file claims for up to $1,000, though the ceiling is as high as $1,500-$2,000 in certain states like New York and California. If the amount owed is more, you can still file in small claims court, but you have to waive anything over the limit-- unless you can find a legitimate way to split up your claim and file separate suits.

For example, if you made two different sales or loans to a person and can show these were two separate transactions, not part of a single agreement, that may qualify you for separate suits. If you have billed someone separately for different products or services--say, one bill for reimbursements, another for services, a third for commissions on sales-- this might qualify for separate suits, too.

Another option, if the amount due is still too little to interest an attorney but over the small claims limit, and if the case is a straightforward one, is to go to municipal court without a lawyer. As long as the case is relatively simple, and you don't have to worry about a lot of legal technicalities or the prospect of confronting an elaborate defense from the debtor, you may be able to do it on your own. (A brief visit with your own attorney to discuss the case beforehand, though, probably would not be a bad investment.)   With a higher debt limit, you would file in superior court instead, though as the amount in question increases, your likelihood of benefiting from a lawyer will, as well. The more money there is at stake, the more likely you are to encounter an attorney on the other side.

In any case, you should be prepared to spend some money and some time. Remember, you'll be compensated for the court fees you pay if you win and collect.

The advantage of small claims court is that it's quick and easy. You file for a few dollars, set a court date, and (barring problems in service or changes in the court date by the defendant), you can be in court in a month or two. The judges are prepared to deal with defendants who aren't lawyers, so you can present your case simply by describing your side of the story. The defendant, if present, gets to give an account of the other side. Finally, the judge may ask some questions, and you'll each have a chance to rebut what the other has said. The whole presentation usually takes a few minutes.

The judge will often give you a decision on the spot. If the case is complicated or the decision is likely to create hostile feelings, the judge will take the matter under advisement; you will probably get the decision by mail in the next day or two.

If the debtor doesn't show up (and many don't--after all, the debtor has already been trying to evade you for months), you need only show enough documents to indicate you have a case, and then you'll almost certainly get a default judgment in your favor. In such a situation, it is common for the judge to give you all that you ask for, as long as he or she feels there is a reasonable, factual basis for your demand. Although there is an appeals process for losing defendants, you rarely have to worry about that. Very few debtors bother to appeal; they know they owe the debt.

Suppose the size of the debt precludes an appearance in small claims court. What then? In municipal or superior court, the process can go as quickly, if the debtor doesn't bother to respond (and many won't). You write up a formal complaint describing your causes of action and request the money due, along with court costs, punitive damages, and other costs deemed proper by the court. After you have the defendant served, he or she has a limited time (usually 30 days) in which to file an answer. If there is a response, a court date is set, and you will have to settle or go to court. Either process can drag on for some time. However, if the defendant doesn't reply, you can ask for a default judgment. Many debtors will be intimidated by the complaint: they may not know what they need to do to answer it, or may realize they cannot win the case. As a result, debtors may fail to respond at this level, as well.

Municipal or superior court can be a quick and easy way of getting justice. It will cost you more to file than in small claims court, typically between $50-$100, but you'll get that back if you win your judgment (and collect).

You must first decide, though, if it's worth the time and effort to go to court. Even if the debtor doesn't respond, you (or an employee who is directly involved with the debt, such as your bookkeeper) must appear in court. In addition, of course, you will have to take the time to file the action and prepare the case. Consider whether it's worthwhile to try to collect in this way when you deduct out the costs for your time and effort. If the debt is under $100, it's probably not. Even if the debt is sizable, ask yourself: would it be more cost-effective to use a collection agency or attorney and get about 50-60% of the total?

You should also consider the matter of collecting after you win. How hard is that going to be? Unless the debtor has assets or is likely to get them in the near future, and you can find them, you are not going to be able to collect for awhile. However, such a judgment is good for a number of years, though the actual periods will vary from state to state. If you are willing to be patient, you may be able to collect down the road.

When should you go to court? The most appropriate circumstances for this type of action are listed below.

(1) The debt is large enough to take the time and effort to go to court yourself, but too small to interest an attorney. (If the debt is over the small claims limit and you want to go to municipal or superior court, the case should be a simple one you can handle on your own.)

(2) You made your final attempt to collect and mediate the case, and are willing to take the chance of irrevocably terminating the relationship by filing suit.

(3) You are willing to invest your energy in preparing for and going to court.

(4) You wish to act quickly, and are uncomfortable with an interim strategy like pre-collection letters or using a collection agency.

(5) You feel that the chance to collect the full amount yourself is worth the effort, and prefer that option to turning the matter over to a collection agency or attorney and getting much less.

Bibliography

For further reference, consult . . .

Advanced Telephone Collecting, American Collectors Association, 1983.

Collection Agency, AEA Business Manual #X1207, American Entrepreneur Association, 1983.

Collection Techniques for Accounts Receivable, T. Frank Hardesty, Dible Management Institute, 1982.

Collection Techniques for the Small Business, Timothy R. Paulson, Self-Counsel Press, 1978.

Complete Credit and Collection Letter Book, John D. Little, Prentice-Hall, 1964.

Credit! Cathy Clark, Eden Press, 1979.

Credit Where Credit is Due, Glen Walker, Holt, Rinehart and Winston, 1979.

Getting Paid, Arnold Goldstein, John Wiley & Sons, 1984.

Handbook of Business Letters, L.E. Frailey, Prentice-Hall, 1984.

Past Due, Norman King, Facts on File, 1983.

Telephone Collectors Handbook, American Collectors Association, 1983.

Your Check is in the Mail, Bruce Goldman and Kenneth Pepper, Warner Books, 1984.